HALF THE WAY HOME

HALF THE WAY HOME

A Memoir of Father
and Son

Adam Hochschild

VIKING

VIKING
Viking Penguin Inc., 40 West 23rd Street,
New York, New York 10010, U.S.A.
Penguin Books Ltd, Harmondsworth,
Middlesex, England
Penguin Books Australia Ltd, Ringwood,
Victoria, Australia
Penguin Books Canada Limited, 2801 John Street,
Markham, Ontario, Canada L3R 1B4
Penguin Books (N.Z.) Ltd, 182–190 Wairau Road,
Auckland 10, New Zealand

First published in 1986 by Viking Penguin Inc.
Published simultaneously in Canada

Portions of this material appeared, in different
form, in *Mother Jones* magazine.

LIBRARY OF CONGRESS CATALOGING IN PUBLICATION DATA
Hochschild, Adam.
Half the way home.
I. Title.
PS3558.O3413H3   1986   813'.54   86-1667
ISBN 0-670-80960-8

Printed in the United States of America by
R. R. Donnelley & Sons Company, Harrisonburg, Virginia
Set in Simonici Life

for Arlie

HALF THE WAY HOME

I

The most vivid memories I have of my childhood are of the summer evenings when Boris's plane took off.

Boris Vasilievich Sergievsky, captain in the Imperial Russian Air Force, World War I fighter ace, winner of the St. George's Cross (which entitles the bearer to a personal audience with the Tsar, any time of day or night), test pilot for the Pan American Clippers of the thirties, tenor, gourmet, lover, horseman, and adventurer, was, miraculously, my uncle. One day he had flown his plane down from the sky and, to the complete shock of all her relatives, had married my father's sister, Gertrude. She was then forty-one years old and had almost certainly never even kissed a man before in her life. From that point on, life in our family was never the same.

Gertrude, my father, and their brother all spent the summer with their families on a large estate called Eagle Nest, in the Adirondack Mountains of upstate New York. When I was a boy, in the years right after World War II, Boris was retired from test piloting. He now operated an air charter business in New York City, flying people anywhere they wanted to go in a ten-passenger Grumman Mallard that could put down on land or water. During the summer, Boris spent his work weeks in New York; for the weekend, he flew north to join his family. Then, on Sunday evenings, with a planeload of houseguests also returning to the city, he took off for New York.

First a crew of workmen used Jeep, winches, and a huge set of dollies for the landing gear to maneuver the plane out of its lakeside hangar and onto a concrete apron. A short time later more people began to arrive: passengers, families, friends, and spectators, coming by motorboat over the lake, or by horseback, car, or station wagon on the mile-long road that ran through the woods to the hangar.

When his passengers had climbed on board, Boris warmed up the plane's engines on shore, watched by a cluster of admiring children. I knelt with my fingers in my ears, a few feet away from the right wing tip. Through the cockpit window I could see the intent faces of Boris and his co-pilot. Their eyes checked instruments on the panel; their lips moved in a mysterious technical jargon I could not hear; their hands reached up to adjust a wondrous galaxy of switches and levers. First one motor, then the other, gave out a long, shattering roar so loud you felt as if you were standing inside the noise. The aircraft rocked and strained at its wheels; the saplings at the edge of the forest behind it bent toward the ground. Finally the engines quieted to a powerful whoosh, and, like an ungainly three-legged duck, the plane rolled down the beach into the water.

Boris taxied out to the middle of the lake, the propellers blowing a wet wind back over us on shore. Suddenly a great white tail of spray spread out behind the plane. The Mallard, its wheels now folded into its belly, lifted higher and higher in the water, transformed into a shape of sleek grace. A motorboat or two raced alongside, then were quickly left behind. At last, triumphantly, the plane broke free of the water and rose into the dusk. The engines' roar echoed off the lake; the very mountains vibrated. A plume of water drops still trailed from the fuselage, then faded to a fine mist, then to nothing. On the ground, people quietly began talking again, moving slowly, reluctantly, toward the waiting cars. High in the sky, Boris dipped a wing and turned toward New York.

It would be tempting to linger on Boris, for his is the easy story to tell. Another's is much harder. Look more closely now at the people mounting the steps into the plane. They turn and wave from the cabin door, then duck their heads and step inside. Here is Boris with his square Russian face and hearty laugh; here is his co-pilot Elmourza Natirboff, a strapping, dashingly handsome young man with jet-black hair and a warm grin; here are laughing guests in brightly colored sport shirts or sweaters, carrying tennis rackets and golf clubs back to the city. And here, the last in line, politely letting the others go first, the only person wearing a suit and tie, is a stocky, broad-shouldered man with a shy, tense, embarrassed smile, ill-at-ease as he always is at any occasion when emotion is to be shown, even a simple weekly farewell. This book is the story of him and me, from those summer Sunday evenings when I waved good-bye to him, and was secretly relieved to see him go, until I held his hand as he died and then was apart from him at last. He is my father.

My father. I always spoke of him, talked to him, thought of him that way. I never called him Dad or Daddy, only, in an awkward way, unlike any other child I knew, Father. There was always a stiffness in the air between us, as if we were both guests at a party and the host had gone off somewhere before introducing us. We never spoke about our relationship with each other, ever.

But sometimes, in those uncomfortable silences, I greatly feared that he might do so, and that he might start by inviting me to call him by a less formal name. As if he were indirectly suggesting this, at times I heard him say to someone else in my hearing, "How's your dad?" But he never did ask me, and I never volunteered. And so he remained, until the end, Father.

I was an only child. What few friends I had were usually so awed by being invited to fly to the Adirondacks on Boris's plane or to travel abroad with us that they never said anything critical of Father. To my mother, he was the most wonderful man in the world, a man who could do no wrong. I never heard her find fault with him or disagree with him in any way. And so for many years it was unimaginably hard for me to do so.

Father was, I thought as a child, a man of vast endurance. I was sure my own body could never become so strong. Whenever we were at Eagle Nest he rode horseback through the woods for many miles each day. In the summers he swam across our lake and back every evening, more than half a mile in all. Until he was nearly fifty, once a summer he swam a six-mile course through a chain of lakes. And he boxed. With a punching bag, with an instructor at his club gym in New York, and, from the time I was five or six on, with me.

He always initiated it: "Adam, do you want to box?"

" . . . O.K.," I replied, feeling that constant uneasiness.

"How about this afternoon at three o'clock?" Everything in his life was by appointments, for which Father was always precisely on time.

" . . . O.K." I didn't like the boxing, but I could never think of a plausible reason to say no. And he never learned, never took the hint, from the fact that *I* never suggested that we box.

At three o'clock we put on our gloves. For him boxing was not an art, a game, or a chance to vent aggression playfully. It was instead a chance to exercise his upper-body muscles. Everything was broken into prescribed movements; every punch fell into categories on a list in his head. He called them out:

"Right to the body! Left to the jaw! . . . No, turn your fist, like *this*. Harder! Left hook! Good! Left to the body! Hard as you can!" His body was like brick: I did hit as hard as I could, and he seemed to feel nothing. "Right hook! Right to the jaw! Good!"

Then there was a brief period of free-for-all boxing, with no called-out instructions. He never hit me hard. My punches just bounced off him. Sometimes we would go into a clinch—half-clinch, half-hug—as if only in the midst of this stylized conflict could we allow ourselves a gesture of affection.

"That's enough for today," Father said. Then, removing his gloves, he offered his cheek down to be kissed, not in celebration of something fun we had done together, but rather to be thanked, for something he had done for me.

When I grew a little older, I saw that Father was shorter than most other men, although he had wide shoulders and immense stamina. Even as he aged, women always found something virile about him. He drank generous quantities, usually vodka, without ever getting the least bit drunk; I several times saw him consume an entire bottle of champagne at one sitting, without showing any effect. All his sports, even the boxing, he did slowly: the swimming was unhurried and deliberate, the horseback riding usually at a trot or walk. When younger friends swam across the lake with him on those summer evenings, they always left him far behind, but he did not mind.

A short man, thus, but sturdy and strong, with small, round, rimless spectacles that glinted in the light, and a cultivated, grammatically correct speech, with every "who" and "whom" in place, a speech sprinkled with slight pauses in which he chose precisely the right word or made sure he was citing exactly the correct date. A voice that had in it not the sound of money, as Gatsby said of Daisy, but of wealth, which is something different: more enduring, more secure, inextricably connected with land, stretching forward and back in time.

Oddly, despite his systematic exercising, Father used a car to go the 150 or so yards between the large building at Eagle Nest where we ate with our guests and the smaller cottage where he and my mother and I slept. Yet he was never comfortable with anything mechanical, and never really got the knack of driving. He stalled frequently, shifted impatiently from first to third gear, or roared forgetfully along at fifty miles an hour in second. Many times, even at low speeds, he skidded off the road in winter, saved from injury only by the high Adirondack snowbanks.

Father's whole existence seemed regulated not by appetites but by will. He had a lifelong ability to take catnaps of predetermined length. "I'm going to sleep for ten minutes," he would say, glancing at his watch. Punctually, ten minutes later, he would wake up. Until he was in his early thirties, he was some fifty pounds overweight.

He decided one day to take it off, asked a doctor what was the correct weight for his size, and for the rest of his life kept his weight within a few pounds of that mark. For some years he smoked cigarettes, but in order not to smoke too much, he simply decided never to smoke before 6 p.m. And, checking his watch once or twice as that hour approached, he never did.

Despite being often ill-at-ease with people, Father seldom noticed that others were aware of his eccentricities. If, for example, he took one of his ten-minute catnaps when on an airplane, he blotted out the light by tearing a newspaper into strips, folding the strips into thick little squares, and wedging them between his glasses and his eyelids. It stopped traffic in the aisles; flight attendants and passengers turned and stared. But he didn't notice; he was asleep.

Father planned all his activities elaborately, and always assumed everything was proceeding according to schedule. So much so that he sometimes ignored signs that it wasn't, especially if I was the one who pointed them out. Once we were both being driven in his limousine from Eagle Nest down the New York State Thruway to Manhattan. We stopped for gas; getting back on the Thruway our family chauffeur took the wrong entrance ramp and headed north instead of south. I was doubly sure of this when the setting sun appeared squarely on our left instead of our right. I timidly pointed this out to Father:

"Look, the sun's over there. I think we made a wrong turn."

"No . . . I'm sure we'll be all right."

"But, Father, the sun sets in the *west*."

He shrugged, mumbled something, and went back to

reading a book. He had bought the best limousine, hired the best chauffeur—bringing him over from England, in fact—how could anything go wrong? He still refused to believe we had made a wrong turn, and was startled when, some time later, the car turned around.

II

In trying to understand Father, his place in the world, and the background against which my relationship with him was played out, I have found myself following several threads backwards in time and space. One, Boris's, leads to an airplane flight on a summer day in 1930. Another thread leads to a Jewish schoolboy in Germany, doing his homework on an evening in the 1870s. And one thread leads to a prospector, tramping through the African bush at the turn of the century.

On the great central plateau of Africa, elephants and buffalo once roamed among forests of scrub trees and high red ant hills. Until early in this century, there were few European settlers. Late one afternoon in 1902, a lone white prospector, hunting for food, shot a roan antelope in a clearing on the banks of the Luanshya River. The animal fell against an outcropping of rock. The next morning the prospector noticed a telltale trace of green embedded in the stone. Extending thousands of feet into the earth below lay what was to prove one of the world's richest deposits of copper. The prospector staked his claim, but the land was sold and resold, and it was to be others who reaped its bounty.

Sixty years later, in the country which today is Zambia,

Father and I descend into the depths of Roan Antelope Mine. We have been given long white coats to wear, and miners' helmets with electric lamps on top. Why the white coats, like doctors'? There is an antiseptic feel about them, as if we are to be protected, set apart, from something messy going on around us: a white coat shows that you are supposed to remain clean. Other white men in white coats lead us along underground corridors of the mine, shouting above the din of drills and jackhammers and ore-carts rumbling along rails.

We pass gangs of black workers in boots and jump suits, being ordered about by white foremen. It is ferociously hot. Sweat makes rivulets in the coating of rock dust on the miners' foreheads. Their eyes stare at us, long and curiously. Later, at another mine, as I watch exhausted miners gulp down enormous platefuls of food, I hear a white official say, "We feed these chaps *well—* four thousand calories a day." Food is fuel.

Our visit belowground does not last long; an elevator whisks us back up to the surface. We visit vast rooms full of roaring furnaces, out of which pour golden spark-showers of molten metal. Cooled into slabs, the copper will travel by rail and ship halfway around the world, to a refinery in New Jersey. After the morning's tour, we have lunch at a Company "guesthouse" with a man whom I last saw one snowy New Year's at Eagle Nest. In one of the company towns that now dot this region, there is a street called Hochschild Crescent; other streets, shafts, mines, and, in another country, a town itself are all named after mining executives we know, family friends whose children I have played with at Eagle Nest, who arrived for the weekend on Boris's plane.

Over lunch at the guesthouse, a black servant silently puts hot plates on the starched white tablecloth. With one ear I hear white officials with British or South African accents: " . . . opening up that new ore body off the north shaft . . . "; " . . . fine new chap in tech training now . . . "; " . . . the union'll be very sticky over the new job classifications. . . . " But my mind is drawn away from the table, back to those few moments of exchanged looks with the black miners, the whites of their eyes standing out in grimed faces beneath helmets, in the heat, thousands of feet under the earth. What was said in those glances between us, with no time to talk, and no language in common? Those men then made only a few shillings a day; I knew, and in an inchoate way, without any clear images to accompany the feeling, I think *they* knew, that their labor, translated into stockholders' dividends and executive salaries and directors' fees, subdividing among subsidiaries and holding companies, finally flowed across the ocean, an invisible ribbon of metal that shaped itself into Eagle Nest.

But back there, all this was never discussed in such terms. In each of Eagle Nest's many bedrooms paneled in rough-cut knotty pine, there was only one sign of that ribbon of metal, only one piece of evidence for the prosecution: a burnished, reddish-brown paperweight a few inches long, a miniature ingot of copper.

Father's father had been one of the founders of the corporation that controlled that mine. It bought the land and began digging several decades after the prospector shot the antelope. Father eventually headed the firm for some years, as did his younger brother after him. In the half-century Father worked for it, the corporation changed its name several times—The American Metal Company, American Metal Climax, AMAX—merged, sold off chunks of its business, and bought up others. Actually, the mines in Africa and Mexico and Colorado, the office Father worked at during frequent visits to London, the ore-carrying ships and the smelters, mostly belonged to subsidiaries or affiliates or joint ventures with other corporations. But still, around the house everyone referred to the whole network as "The Company."

Surprisingly, however, no one referred to it very much. Partly because of the taboo on discussing the source of one's wealth, but more so because, despite his success at it, Father was basically not interested in business. He read *The New York Times* every day with a thoroughness that bordered on the obsessional, but barely glanced at the business pages. His secretary clipped for him *The Wall Street Journal*'s articles on international politics; he ignored the rest. When younger men from The Company and their families were our guests for weekends at Eagle Nest, an invisible telegraph passed along to them the message that Harold Hochschild did not talk business at home.

Occasionally the telegraph failed. Once an eager young executive at our house for dinner said, "Isn't it marvelous what copper prices have been doing lately!" Father gave him a freezing look and changed the subject.

The Company bought and sold metals, and invested in mines all over the world. But in the 1950s, when I was growing up, copper was its heart. The bulk of this metal came from the Copperbelt of central Africa. This small swath of what was then Northern Rhodesia and the Belgian Congo and is now Zambia and Zaire is a thick, deep, underground river of copper ore. Cities grew atop it, for by the time a mine is sunk and miners and their families settle there, one mine may have twenty or thirty thousand people living on the ground above. All these details remained hazily in the background as I grew up. Father "went out," as the British said, to Africa twice a year, visited the mines, and came back to talk about the continent's physical beauty, the hidebound conservatism of the white colonists, the segregationist labor laws he was trying to get changed, the excitement of new nations coming into being, but seldom of the business itself.

As a child I knew only that The Company, like a vast but invisible labyrinth, underlay all we had. We traveled a good deal on my school vacations, and everywhere we went—Sweden, Germany, Argentina—the local man from The Company, its sales agent in countries where it did not have mines, always met us. We would get off the plane or the ship, and while we stood in the customs line, a smiling man would wave and beckon from the other side of the barrier. He knew someone, or had tipped someone, or had simply *told* someone. A special door would open; the man would usher us to a hidden lounge. "Hello, Mr. and Mrs. Hochschild! And you must be young Adam!"

The smiling man would take us in his charge; we would meet his family. His wife would make us "a real Argentine (or Swedish, or German) dinner"; his teenage son would make conversation with me; the smiling man would make sure that at our hotel there would be fruit and flowers waiting "with the compliments of the management." But he, too, had been warned, and business was never discussed.

I still half expect a smiling man to be there anytime I arrive in a new country. Even if I were on a plane that had been hijacked, with all the passengers held at gunpoint, a hand would quietly take my bag, a voice would say, "You don't have to stay with the others, Mr. Hochschild. Come right this way. . . . "

· · ·

Some six years before Father was born, his own father had come to the United States. For him, too, there may have been a smiling man on the other side of the customs barrier. For although Berthold Hochschild arrived in 1886, at the beginning of the great wave of Jewish immigrants from Europe, he traveled first-class. He felt no kinship, so far as I can tell, with the hundreds of thousands of other Jews who soon filled New York's Lower East Side. They spoke Yiddish and kept kosher; he spoke German and had a Christmas tree. They were Eastern European; he was from Germany. They dealt with fellow laborers or small shopkeepers; the business he worked for depended on loans from Gentile investment bankers like the Morgans. The gulf between Berthold and most American Jews was enormous, and he preferred to keep it that way. So, as I was to discover gradually over the years, did his son, Father.

Berthold had been sent to New York by a German metals trading company to help set up a U.S. affiliate. This he did, but by the time two world wars had redistributed the globe's wealth in America's favor, The Company had long become independent. Officially, The Company began on the day when Berthold Hochschild and his associates signed the incorporation papers. But I think it really began a decade earlier, when he was still a teenager in the small farming village (which today also has its Hochschildstrasse) near Frankfurt where his family kept cows and ran a grain and feed store.

In one of Berthold's old school copybooks, page after page is filled with dutiful exercises in the old German formal script. Then you turn the page, and abruptly, like a sudden vista as a road rounds the side of a mountain, the book explodes into a magnificent chart that spreads across two whole pages, obviously done with love and care and far more detail than the teacher asked for. Or perhaps the teacher didn't ask for it at all, for it is not usual school subject matter. Along the top and side of the chart are listed all the currencies of the known world: marks, dollars, pesos, francs, pounds, kroner, lire, imperial rubles, and so on. The chart shows how each converts into every other one, at the current rates of exchange. Then, on the following page, the exercises in the Gothic handwriting resume. I imagine the evening Berthold worked on that chart—kerosene lamp lighting the family kitchen, the cows chewing hay in the barn next door—as the moment when, in his mind, The Company was born.

Berthold was not the only Hochschild with visions of dollars and pesos. One relative went to Baltimore and started a large department store. Three other cousins from Berthold's own village went to South America and got rich in the mining business in Bolivia and Chile. One of these converted to Roman Catholicism, and his wife began signing their name *de* Hochschild. Somehow all the Hochschilds seem to have known that in any catastrophe the smiling man at the airport would appear at the right moment. We lost no close relatives in the Holocaust. Almost everybody was able to leave Germany in time. One cousin, who was married to a Gentile, stayed—and, astoundingly, survived unharmed. The Nazis made her wear the yellow star and work in a factory. But a friendly official in her town kept ignoring the paperwork ordering her to a concentration camp. And she was driven to the factory job by the family chauffeur.

III

There could be no more improbable addition to our family than Boris Sergievsky. He flew into the life of the Hochschilds a dozen years before I was born. Someone had suggested to Father and his brother, Walter, that they buy a small seaplane with which to commute the 220 miles between Manhattan and Eagle Nest on summer weekends. They called the Sikorsky aircraft company. The country was then in the Great Depression, and the company was so eager to sell a plane that it said it would send its chief pilot to fly Father and Walter from New York to Eagle Nest as a free demonstration. And so Boris descended out of the clouds and saw a large country home like those of his beloved pre-Revolutionary Russia, and, among the crowd of curious onlookers gathered on shore to meet the plane, an unmarried sister.

Gertrude was then in her late thirties. Until his death two years before, she had devoted herself largely to taking care of Berthold, her aging father. She had had no boyfriends. Even more than Father, she was immensely formal: people who knew her in college say she seldom went out socially, always returned home each afternoon, and called fellow students "Mr." and "Miss." A small, reserved woman, she had a slow walk that came from a chronic foot ailment, and a dignified, sad, dark-haired beauty. Something about her face, particularly her luminously intelligent eyes, made her stand out in a group. She always appeared quieter than whomever she was with, and had gentle features that showed insight and wisdom. She liked listening to music, and to the opera, although what she heard there, what it spoke to her of, I did not know, for she never talked about her feelings. Both the depths of those feelings and the barriers around them were always visible: she was, a cousin of mine once said, like a candle inside a block of ice.

Boris's life could not have been more different. As an officer of the Tsar's infantry in World War I, he had won the Empire's highest medal by leading his company of soldiers uphill to capture a fortified mountaintop. Charging over the last wall, they fought hand-to-hand with Austro-Hungarian soldiers, Boris slashing with his sword; his coat was ripped by an enemy bayonet.

Later Boris transferred to the air force, where he commanded a fighter squadron and shot down eleven German planes. During the war, he developed a new method of fighter attack: you approach the enemy plane head-on at a higher altitude, then wing-over quickly and attack from the rear before the German back-seat machine-gunner has time to swivel around and fire at you. By day Boris dueled in the skies; by night he dallied with a contingent of nurses stationed near his airfield. The cook in his squadron mess had been chef of the best restaurant in Kiev.

When the Russian Civil War began, Boris fought on the Tsarist side, both on foot and in the air. He was captured by the Bolsheviks, escaped from prison, worked as a gymnastics instructor in Poland, and made his way to the United States. The first job he could find in New York was with a pick and shovel, digging the Holland Tunnel. Eventually he went to work as test pilot for his old schoolmate, the aircraft designer Igor Sikorsky.

In interludes when there were no new planes to test at the Sikorsky factory, Boris flew oil prospectors up Colombia's turbulent, alligator-ridden Magdalena River into the Andes, and flew cargoes of live boa constrictors downriver, to be made into snakeskin shoes and handbags. His taxiing plane was sunk by a forty-foot tidal wave off the coast of Chile. He flew the Prince of Wales on a tour of South America. He flew with Lindbergh. He took National Geographic Society mapmakers on aerial surveys of remote parts of the globe. In Africa he landed his plane on lakes where no plane had ever landed before; one picture at Eagle Nest showed his aircraft surrounded by a crowd of curious pygmies.

Parts of Boris's past kept surfacing unexpectedly. Once he was giving a talk about his World War I exploits at an aviators' club in New York. He told of the time he had fought one-on-one with a German pilot, then shot the plane down just on the Russian side of the front line. The German pilot crash-landed in a field, then leapt out and began running toward German-held territory, chased by Russian infantrymen. The Russians gained on their quarry, who was encumbered by all his heavy flying gear. He speeded up by casting off his leather coat. The pursuers gained more ground, so the German tore off his flying suit. "And so," Boris concluded, "he escaped across the lines wearing only his underwear!"

In the back of the room, someone slowly rose to his feet and called out in astonishment:

"I vas dat man!"

. . .

For five years after that first meeting at the Eagle Nest lakeside in 1930, Boris courted Gertrude secretly. In his rough-and-tumble way he plowed through any doubts she had. He was not dissuaded by the constant presence of a cousin and close friend Gertrude had adopted as part of her summer household, Hannah Blumenthal. Hannah was a widow some years older than Gertrude, a placid, silver-haired woman whose majestic looks never changed over the years, though she lived to be ninety-nine. Gertrude traveled with Hannah, spent vacations with her, and generally used her as an emotional body-guard. Hannah's constant presence had kept other men away from Gertrude, but to Boris this was just one more hurdle he could leap.

Gertrude did not tell her two brothers that she was continuing to see the Russian pilot of the plane they had years before decided not to buy. Then one day she called Father and Walter at The Company office and said, "I have something I want to tell you both." She took the subway downtown and, to their amazement, informed them, "In two weeks, I'm getting married to Captain Boris Sergievsky."

This, then, is the official story of how Gertrude and Boris married, as told me by my parents. At the core of it, though not spoken aloud, is the implication that he married her for her money—money which did, in fact, set him up royally in champagne, horses, and airplanes for the rest of his life. But there is, if not a contradictory story, another one. Perhaps both are true; I do not know. A few years ago, long after Boris and Gertrude were in their graves, some letters turned up which seemed to show that against all the traditions of her sex, her class, and her family, it was Gertrude who had taken the initiative and asked Boris to marry her.

It warmed me when I heard this: to think of her, alone, telling no one, a forty-one-year-old virgin, embodiment of all the respectability of a deeply repressed family, reaching hesitantly out toward a man who seemed to promise her a more daring life. On her wedding night, it was an entire new world she took into her bed. It was a move of great courage.

Father, however, did not see it that way. Not only was his sister marrying a Russian adventurer who might be after her money, but Boris had been married twice before. To top it off, Boris was late for the wedding because he had to finish off a test-piloting assignment. Father and Gertrude watched his loops and spins from the ground. After the ceremony, the couple departed for a trip to Europe. A photo shows the two of them on skis at St. Moritz. Boris is smiling his usual bluff grin; Gertrude's expression is tense and frozen, a little downcast, as if she is beginning a risky journey and is not at all sure how it will come out.

Not shown in the picture is Hannah Blumenthal, whom, to Boris's surprise, Gertrude invited along on their honeymoon.

IV

When Gertrude married Boris, Father was still a bachelor. In a way, the two of them were still living in the
shadow of their father, who had died a few years earlier.
Father and Gertrude seldom talked about Berthold while
I was growing up. And so my picture of my grandfather
had only a few brushstrokes. Snapshots show him as a
short man with a watch chain and walrus mustache.
Even photographed in a bathing suit, he looks dressed
for a parade. He appears to have been of overpowering
rectitude. Berthold expected complete obedience from
his children, and he got it. His two sons followed him
into The Company; no other choice was even conceiv-
able.

There, Father was extremely successful. He had few
outside interests. Two decades after Berthold's death, he
became chairman of The Company. The position did not
come to him automatically, for the family owned only a
small proportion of the corporation's stock.

The child's-eye view I had of Father's early business
life had almost entirely to do with the countries he went
to, for this is what he talked about. He crossed the con-
tinental divide of the Andes on horseback in 1916, inspected mines in Mexico, and worked nearly a year
trading silver in India. The high point came when he
spent nearly two years in the 1920s as The Company's

representative in China. He took some lessons in the two main dialects of Chinese, and remained intensely interested in the country all his life.

As he sat by the fireplace at Eagle Nest and talked about China, I sometimes wondered what was the source of its fascination for him. He never speculated, so that remained a mystery to me. Was there a woman in China? Or was it that the Far East was as far as he could get from Berthold? Whatever the lure, it was so strong that he planned to retire from business at the age of fifty and live in China for most of each year. Knowing his methodical determination, I'm sure he would have acted on that decision, had he not, when he reached that age in 1942, found himself newly married and the world at war.

While in China he took an enormous dislike to the regime of Chiang Kai-shek. Father tended to make quick, firm, and long-lasting judgments on political figures. He met China's leaders, but, he said, "All Chiang's relatives had their hands in the till. A corrupt family, almost the whole lot of them. The only decent one was Madame Sun Yat-sen."

She eventually sided with the Communists, and so when the Chinese Revolution took place two decades later, Father, in his idiosyncratic way, decided it must be basically a good thing. This was a rare opinion during the 1950s, and many of Father's Establishment friends raised their eyebrows at his repeated letters to *The New York Times* saying that the United States should pull its head out of the sand and recognize "Red China."

Photographs of Father during his thirties show him quite overweight, with a tight, nervous smile. He was always very constrained with women. People remember him as being extremely shy at parties, always standing at the side of the room. He expected to remain single all his life, forever destined to be the unattached extra man at dinner parties. Among his letters is one to a friend, written when he was about thirty, in which Father describes a vacation he is taking at a resort hotel, alone. He lists what he does at various times of day: 8 to 8:30 eat breakfast, 8:30 to 11 a.m. read, 11:00 to 11:30 swim, and so on, until: "from 10 p.m. until midnight I watch people dancing."

Only once, briefly and very haltingly, as if he were forcing himself with great effort to overcome some huge barrier to talking about it, did Father tell me, as we were driving along in the car one day, that he had had a relationship with a woman during those bachelor years, something that lasted on and off for a decade. Whether it was a relationship in the modern, sexual sense of the word, or one that ended each evening as he helped her out of a taxi and kissed her goodnight under the awning of her East Side apartment building, I do not know.

He almost never spoke of anything having to do with sex. There were only two occasions when he even brought up the subject—each time painfully, as if under some difficult obligation that had been on his mind for weeks.

Once it was to say:

"You know, Adam, you're reaching a time of life where . . . there'll be many changes. If you ever have any questions about . . . about such things, I'll be glad to try to answer them."

"O.K.," I mumbled. I already knew the answers by that point, but felt I ought to respond to the effort he was making. Yet his embarrassment was so great that it seemed impossibly difficult for me to ask anything.

The other occasion was again in the enforced intimacy of a long car trip. Abruptly, breaking one of the awkward silences that so often occurred when we were alone together, Father said, apropos of nothing, without taking his eyes from the road in front of him:

"You know, generally I think it's a good thing if people don't sleep together until they get married."

End of discussion. Did Father follow that rule? Until he married at the age of forty-nine? I never dared ask. I was never able to find out.

That one woman he did date before he met my mother was from an old, upper-crust WASP family. With Berthold's urging, Father had set his course early on assimilation. From college on, almost all the friends he made were not Jewish. He moved from the Upper West Side, the heart of New York's German-Jewish community, to the more Gentile Park Avenue. Later, after I was born, Father seldom mentioned our Jewish heritage. It was my Anglo-Saxon mother who repeatedly told me it was something to be proud of.

He met her on the eve of World War II. Coming from a well-to-do Episcopalian family full of Mayflower ancestors, Mary Marquand satisfied the necessary ethnic requirements. But he obviously saw much more in her—and she in him—as well. She was nearly forty and had never been married. On their third date he asked her to marry him. A year and a half later, she did. It was, against all probability, the best marriage I know in their generation.

In what did that love consist? Tolstoy is wrong when he says happy families are all alike; what he should have said, I think, is that they are alike only in being difficult

to describe. The unhappy ones are easier, because griev-
ances loom so large. Differences are always more likely
to be put into words than agreement—with the latter,
why bother? My parents each gave me the feeling that
their marriage was somehow a miraculous, unexpected
windfall in lives that otherwise were destined to be spent
alone. Sexually as well, the two of them must have been
content with each other, but that they kept to themselves; it was always an enigma to me: how could two
such restrained, dignified, and previously inexperienced
people manage at all? Perhaps one necessary ingredient
for lasting love is that you start with an equal level of
repression. Thus, they both blossomed for the first time
together. Years later, my mother, an avid gardener,
wrote several articles for horticultural magazines on
plants that bloom in winter, showing flowers through the
snow.

To picture my mother it is necessary to imagine a tall,
gray-haired woman, a bit regal-looking, but in a benev-
olent way. She is half-sitting, half-lying on the living
room couch with her feet up, a position which, she
quickly explains, is easier on her back, or her legs, or her
headache. Yet despite this constant absorption with her
health, there is something profoundly warm about her.
When she says, "Now tell me about *you*," her interest is
deep and genuine. Her face goes easily into expressive
crinkles of kindness, concern, and laughter in response
to what you say.

My mother could never bring herself to convey bad
news. When that had to be done, she always waited until
Father was home to do it, whether it was a servant to be
fired or a son to be reprimanded. Instead, she took any

opportunity to give support or encouragement. She telephoned or wrote to friends in trouble, telling them she was with them all the way, offering advice or help. Although timid and fearful in many ways herself, this made her still better as an empathic listener and comforter. She believed that enough reassurance would get anyone through any crisis. Her frequent comment about anyone she was trying to help was "Oh, I wish I could give her a self-confidence injection!"

Like almost all the women of her generation, my mother bent her life to fit her husband's. She ran the household when Father was away on business trips. She loyally entertained his friends with Eagle Nest summer weekends even when he was gone during World War II. A painter before she married, good enough to sell some pictures through New York galleries, she readily abandoned her career after I was born. When we sat at the dinner table, she was always the interested listener to Father's opinions on Africa or Truman or MacArthur, drawing him out with encouraging questions. Yet, consciously at least, she did not feel she had made any sacrifices by all this; women with such a perspective were, in my mother's eyes, "career girls," a category of people toward whom she had a sort of puzzled tolerance.

My parents looked an odd match. My mother was several inches taller than Father; he didn't mind, but she was self-conscious about it, she said—although she accentuated the difference by wearing high heels. Her face was long and angular; his, round. She had a majestic head of gray hair; he was bald. He had endless vigor; she tired easily. After an overnight plane trip returning from abroad, he went to the office and boxing gym and theater for a normal day's activities; she went to bed for a day or two to recover. My mother feared germs, disease, dirt;

Father was the most unsqueamish person imaginable. Once while he was away, she wrote him in alarm about mice in the house; he replied cheerfully that he had seen them there too—a mouse had once run across his head during the night, "but he found it rather slippery going and so didn't return."

Their other eccentricities were separate as well, rather than the shared quirks of a couple who met young and grew old together. Yet each adjusted to the other. He tolerated her frequent psychosomatic maladies without complaint; she accepted his difficulty in expressing his feelings with the faith that they lay there, nonetheless, underneath.

Father dreaded birthdays, anniversaries, or any other occasions when public emotion was called for. When returning from his twice-a-year trips to Africa, where he was often gone a month or more, he grew impatient with greetings when we came to meet him at the airport, and wanted instead to look at his mail. Eventually my mother took to bringing it along for him to read on the drive home. His emotions showed only through the cracks. Once the three of us were at Eagle Nest, all reading after dinner one winter evening while a fire blazed. For a few seconds Father lowered his *New York Times,* and said, "You know, there isn't anywhere in the world I'd rather be than right *here.*" Then he picked up the paper and resumed reading. My mother treasured the moment for years.

Her great dream in life had always been to have children. When she thought she was never going to marry, she tried to adopt a child, something highly unusual for a single, upper-class woman in the 1930s. U.S. adoption agencies insisted on two parents; she had started to talk to agencies in Canada when she met Father. I arrived a year after they were married, when she was forty-two. When she became pregnant she told friends, "I feel like riding around New York on buses so the whole world can see."

Visiting children always knew they could come to my mother for cookies, time, attention, some special toy brought out of hiding, and the assurance, expressed by a conspiratorial wink, that she would far rather be talking to them than to their parents. She once did some marvelous illustrations for an unpublished children's book; they show the whole world from the perspective of a two-year-old: people seen only from the knees down, with shoes as big as boulders.

That same ability to identify whimsically with the underdog showed up in my mother's other drawings and paintings. The best of them were not the landscapes or formal portraits on which she spent the most time but the quick, humorous sketches she did on sudden impulse. My favorite shows an outdoor riding ring where the bleachers are filled with seated horses, who are kissing, drinking soda pop with straws, and loosing colored balloons to the sky while they watch men in top hats and red tailcoats, riding each other, leap the hurdles of a steeplechase.

V

My parents were on their honeymoon, swimming in a Guatemalan lake, when a voice on the radio carried out over the water the news that Pearl Harbor had been bombed. They hurried home. An Eagle Nest boyhood playmate who was in Roosevelt's cabinet asked Father to come to Washington as an Assistant Secretary of the Treasury, but he declined. Instead Father spent much of the next year trying to get into uniform—a difficult proposition at the age of fifty. Thinking it might help, he studied Russian; he had always been fascinated with languages, although he had a rather poor ear for them. Father's eagerness to be in the military came partly from a genuine anger at Hitler and partly from an urgent, anxious desire to prove, as he several times told me later, that "Jews could do their part."

After months of pulling strings in Washington, Father succeeded in his efforts, and he was commissioned into the Army as a major. He went away for training, returning home only for weekends, and then, in the spring of 1943, only a year and a half after his marriage, he sailed for England. There and, after D-Day, in France, he commanded an intelligence unit attached to Eisenhower's headquarters.

I was only a baby when Father left for the war, but from his description I have a vivid picture. He boards the

Queen Mary. Blacked out to hide from German subma-
rines, the great ship slips out of New York harbor at
night. Fifteen thousand soldiers are crammed on board,
far more than there are lifeboats for. But the ship avoids
subs by outrunning them, steaming at top speed on a zig-
zag course across the Atlantic.

The first night Father goes to the first-class lounge
after dinner. Although he is in uniform, a steward rec-
ognizes him from earlier crossings, says, "Good evening,
sir," and confides despairingly how masses of raw American troops are ruining the great ship. Father chats with
him awhile, then returns to the cabin he has to share with
three other majors. They have never been on an ocean
liner before, and complain about everything. Here Father's picture ceases, and I can only imagine. I see his
nervous smile, his uncomfortableness with the Army
slang and profanity and with his roommates, who are all
much younger than he. They chew gum; one or two are
Midwesterners who've hardly ever seen a Jew before. But
I picture him going to sleep happy. He has succeeded. He
has not missed out on the great event of his generation.
He is doing his part.

For two years I was alone with my anxious mother,
who was helped by a chain of nurses and governesses.
Then came a time when every day for weeks she told me,
"Your father is coming home!" until the word "father"
was fixed in my mind with the aura of a long-awaited toy
or birthday present.

Instead, a husky stranger in an Army uniform turned
up on the doorstep, took my mother off for a long weekend, and returned to claim our New York apartment and
Eagle Nest as his own. For years afterward I played endlessly with toy soldiers and looked at picture books of
World War II, following its course from the first Stukas

diving down on Warsaw until the raising of the red flag over the Reichstag. Why? Maybe I wanted the war to start once more, and to take him away again.

Two years after the war ended, Father was made head of The Company. He worked long hours. Except for a few minutes at breakfast and bedtime, I saw him only on weekends. And then, in his attempts to get to know me, he proceeded with the same relentless, methodical determination he applied to everything in life.

"Adam, guess what we're going to do this Saturday!"

"What?" I began to feel a cold, nervous dread.

"I thought we'd drive down and take a ride on the Staten Island Ferry. O.K.?"

" . . . well, O.K." I hoped some last-minute crisis would make the trip impossible, but that never happened.

Instead, as my mother was putting me to bed she would say: "Isn't Father *nice* to plan a special trip just for you and him!"

"Mummy, I don't want to go. Can't *you* come?"

"No, this is something special just for the two of you. For boys only!"

Saturday morning she saw us off, still the cheerleader for our togetherness:

"Now you boys have a good time together!"

The apartment building's doorman went to the garage to fetch Father's car, a huge, gray, bulbous 1940 Cadillac convertible. We got in; the car's windows were far above my head. I was walled into a menacing space I could not see out of: at my eye level were only the radio, the glove compartment, Father's broad chest.

"Are you having a good time, Adam?"

"Yes. . . . Sure."

"Shall we stop for a hamburger or something?"

"I'm not too hungry."

At the ferry I smiled and grinned as I was supposed to; sometimes I actually did enjoy the places we went to. Father had systematically inventoried the unusual outdoor spots a boy might like around New York: the Brooklyn Bridge, the piers, the overpass at Spuyten Duyvil where you could watch the New York Central trains rush past beneath you. But the bridges and ferries failed to connect us. I always felt as if I were holding my breath until we got home.

When we did, he said, "Well, you had a good time, didn't you?"

This was my cue to say thank you, and to give him the kiss that symbolized my gratitude. Being thanked was urgently important to Father. I think he also had the unspoken hope that on one of these trips I would say "I'm glad we did this" or "I love you." I seldom gave him that satisfaction; my taciturn resistance was the only weapon I had against him. When I sometimes slipped in my stubbornness, I knew it registered, for I would hear from my mother, always the eager intermediary, "Father was *so* pleased yesterday when you put your arm around him." Such moments were rare.

One day when I am five years old I get an earache that does not go away. My whole head hurts. A few days later pus and blood begin to stream out of my ear. If I touch that side of my head, it sounds as if I am underwater, hearing the sound of rocks dully clinking against each other. There are many visits to the doctor; my mother bundles me into taxicabs, reassuring, comforting. And she takes me to a whole array of doctors. I have learned the way, though, to the main one, Dr. Haas, our pediatrician, and I always start to cry when the taxi is two or three blocks away.

Doctors' offices in Manhattan are often on the basement floor of old brownstones, so you must go down a few steps, as if entering a cellar. The doctors pull their shades so that people passing on the sidewalks above can't look in; when the rooms then become darkened, the doctors have gooseneck lamps on their desks which throw the light down on their papers, and, by reflection, up, illuminating their faces from the bottom, like those of people in horror movies.

In one such ghostly office there is a giant model of the human ear, with the parts painted in different colors. And a doctor who, unlike the others, wears a round mirror on his forehead, a glinting, sinister device of unknown purpose. When he bends over me, frowning, I can see black hairs bristling from inside his nostrils.

After examining me, he confers with my mother, alone.

At home that night my parents talk behind the closed door of their bedroom.

The next morning my mother explains:

"You're going to be going someplace where they'll put you to sleep, dear. Then they can take out the bad stuff that's hurting you. They'll just give you a little gas, and you won't feel anything."

"Put to sleep, Mummy? Like dogs and cats when they get old?"

"No, dear, not like that . . . "

"Gas—like gas in the car?"

It all takes much explaining.

When the day for the operation comes, I first imagine that we will go back to one of those ghostly basement offices, and that whatever the ghosts will do to me will be by the light of a gooseneck lamp. But no. We head in another direction. And they are both taking me, not just her. For Father to stay home from work on a weekday and do something with me was unheard-of; I vaguely imagine mines and smelters resting idle in his absence. He stands in my playroom, smiling nervously, wearing a blue pinstripe suit, with a coat over his arm, waiting for me as my governess helps me get dressed. Waiting . . . to take me where? Even though my mother, my protector, is with us too, the whole experience is already linked in my mind with the idea of *his* taking me somewhere for something sinister to be done to me.

The hospital room is small, dark, with a window that opens onto a brick-walled air shaft, as if I am in prison. In the bathroom, some enamel has chipped off the tub, exposing a long rusty scar of metal. The scar seems menacing, so unlike the sleek white tubs at home. My mother goes off to talk to the doctor. The hospital smells strangely, of alcohol and disinfectant. The nurse doesn't know our family words for using the toilet; when I say I have to go, she doesn't understand. I begin to cry.

The pain in my ear is worse, a relentless buildup of pressure. My mother tries to stay with me the whole time; she even gets a cot and sleeps in the room. But they won't let her come when they take me away for the operation. Wheeled down the corridor, I am alone in the realm of the ghosts, who now wear green-white gowns. It is all frighteningly different from how she had said it would be: taking the anesthetic does not feel like going to sleep; it feels like being dragged ever more rapidly along a bumpy road, under a whirling, roaring night sky that finally collapses onto me.

When I wake up, it doesn't hurt less, it hurts more. My

entire head is bandaged. It feels as if it will burst. I am ravenously thirsty, but for some reason am not allowed to drink. When my mother had said I would "wake up" after the operation, I had expected to wake up at home, in my own bed, where I always wake up. But I am still in the treacherous, strange-smelling hospital. I cry without ceasing. It is night. They turn off a light to try to make me sleep. Nurses bustle in and out, dark, flitting figures visible through a fog of pain. My mother hovers nearby, conferring with them, soothing me. Finally someone compounds the hurt by giving me a shot of something with a sharp needle. As I cry, a voice says, "I think he'll sleep now."

I stay in the hospital a week. More doctors, more medicines, more pain. I had been right: it *had* been dangerous to leave the house with Father.

My mother still sleeps on the cot beside me, but for a few hours each day she leaves the hospital, to return to our apartment or to do errands. That is the worst time. Lying alone in the room, I can hear the footsteps of visitors coming down the hall, before they reach the door. Of Helene, my governess at the time, a high-heeled spinsterly clop-clop of legs in a tight skirt taking short steps. A neutral feeling: she won't harm me, she is on my side. But then the heavy, slower, heel-toe, heel-toe step that is *his,* Father's, heralded by a hospital nurse's saying brightly, "There's someone special here to see you!" What will happen *now*? My stomach tightens. Yet even here I have to smile, to pretend to be glad to see him. We talk for a few minutes as awkwardly as usual; luckily he does not stay long. And then at last, returning, my mother's step—high heels also, but the steps a split second farther apart because of her height, a brisk, warm, comforting step. I can relax. I am safe again.

Somewhere in that week they try to make me swallow penicillin: a chalky, powdery liquid, white like the hospital sheets and beds and uniforms. It feels poisonous, nauseating. I gag, and from then on they give it to me in shots instead.

The operation had been performed to remove an infected piece of the mastoid bone of my ear, an unusual and fairly serious procedure. For my mother, my illness confirmed her instinctive vision of the great pool of disease on all sides that threatened everyone, especially her and me. She kept me home from school for the rest of the year.

Despite all the reassuring things people told me, I knew that a part of my body had been taken away. I was afraid that whoever had removed it would return, and take me through all that pain and whiteness again. Strange places of any kind became laden with danger.

On the first day of school the next fall, I went to the room I remembered, the familiar place. Several teachers laughed at me:

"Adam, this is the kindergarten! You're in first grade now."

I cried uncontrollably.

The next morning at school I again broke into a paroxysm of crying. The school called home, and my governess came in a taxi to pick me up.

The following morning I began crying at home. My mother was surprised but sympathetic:

"What's the matter, dear?"

I tried in vain to explain.

"Adam, I'm sure you'll feel all right once you get

there," said Father impatiently. "Pull yourself together now. Come on, I'll take you."

Sick with nameless fear, I was led by him out the door. In the apartment building's lobby, I vomited.

The next day I pleaded desperately with my mother to come to school with me. And, mercifully, understandingly, she did. Every day for some weeks she stayed with me for the first hour or so. She sat quietly at the side of the classroom and left, with a quick smile at the teacher, only when it was clear I would be all right.

My greatest fear of all in those years, which I never dared voice to anyone, was that she would die and I would be left alone with Father. She was the one person who could explain to the rest of the world that I needed special treatment. Once that fear overcame me in first-grade music class and I broke down. For the next several years I ran crying and nauseated from rooms, restaurants, airport lounges, every time I heard music. My mother spoke to somebody, and for two years I didn't have to take music at school.

Pictures of me from that time show a thin, somber boy in too-baggy pants and a narrow-brimmed corduroy cap. Usually I am holding a teddy bear or some other talisman. Often I am somewhere where I am supposed to be having a good time, as people always are in family photos: a party, a mountaintop, a beach. Sometimes someone is nudging me to smile at the camera. In cold weather, I always have one more layer of clothing—earmuffs, scarf, mittens—than anyone else in the picture.

The weekend excursions with Father continued. Since I was older and supposedly more mature, these trips now became, frighteningly, overnight ones. They were always introduced with great fanfare, after advance buildup from my mother, as surprise presents. We went to places like Niagara Falls or Montreal or Washington, D.C. I always felt a clammy fear departing on these trips: I would be alone with him for two days in a strange place. My mother would not be there. It was always a vast relief to get home.

Part of my fear had to do with the hospital. Then, too, it had been Father who had taken me away, and something terrible had happened. On these trips, I feared it would happen again. I had a vivid dream at this time: I was alone with Father on a desolate road, somewhere outside New York, in the old gray Cadillac. We stopped at a gas station; he got out and disappeared. Then suddenly the face of the gas station attendant—or was it Father's, transformed?—pressed against the back window: an appalling face, dark-browed, glaring, bristling with black beard stubble. I woke up screaming in terror.

I developed various phobias; the main one was about food. An echo, perhaps, of that liquid penicillin I had gagged on in the hospital. The fear grew steadily worse: an aversion to milky, whitish foods like eggs or yogurt or pudding, a sudden stomach-fluttering queasiness that spread through my whole body when I was about to eat in a strange place, usually a restaurant. I had these attacks often, but they were most likely to occur when it was time for me to sit down for a meal alone with Father, on one of those trips away from home. I wished passionately that I could control the nausea, turn it off with a switch, but I could not. I can still remember things that I ate, or that Father urged me to eat, in different hotel dining rooms.

"Come on, Adam, have some of your steak now. It's getting cold."

"I don't want to."

"But I thought you *liked* steak. That's why I ordered it for you."

"I don't want to."

"I want you to eat just one bite. It's important." His lips pursed: he had brought me all this way, given up his weekend for me; what a neurotic, ungrateful boy.

"I *can't.*" I was on the verge of crying. I was hundreds of miles away from home, trapped, a soldier behind enemy lines.

Sometimes he insisted, and I was sick to my stomach; sometimes he just grew exasperated, and the cloud of his annoyance hung over the rest of the day. He could not understand. I lacked words to explain. For years I was to feel that cold clutch of dread in my stomach when sitting across a restaurant table from him, or from someone who reminded me of him.

All this was made worse by Father's own eating habits, which could not have been more different from mine. His stomach was steel. He liked raw hamburger, raw oysters, raw eggs. He preferred all meat cold. His favorite food was two-inch-thick steak, which he ate barely cooked or sometimes completely raw, fat and all. And he loved dining out. He knew chefs, waiters, maître d's everywhere. He tipped well. He always gave careful instructions about just how rare he wanted his steak, in English and French (*bleu*!). He studied menus and offered his guests suggestions, always the most expensive items: "Why don't you try the lobster?" or "The pâté here is excellent," and "You'll have an appetizer, of course? And a soup?" Oddly, he did not really savor good food himself; he ate quickly and was pleased more by the expensiveness of a dish than by its actual taste. But he wanted his guests in a restaurant to enjoy their food, to be thrilled at the lavishness of it, and, above all, to be grateful afterward. I so dreaded that pressure from him that it took me years to see all the fears of his own that lay hidden behind it.

VI

Although we lived elsewhere during the school year, and were at Eagle Nest for only two or three months a year, it was then that I lived; all else was waiting. As I grew older I came to see that Eagle Nest was more than just a beloved vacation spot or the colorful backdrop to my relationship with Father. It was part of him, a way of life of his own creation.

One can approach Eagle Nest from many vantage points: that of a visiting official from a Company mine on a distant continent, nervously planning opening lines of polite conversation to try with Father; or that of a local woman working in the kitchen, looking out through the pantry door at the array of guests from all over the world; or that of an excited child, peering out of a car window at the start of a weekend's visit, warned by parents to be on best behavior. Let us try approaching, however, from the air, with Boris Sergievsky on that day in 1930, twelve years before I was born, when he flies up from New York in the Sikorsky S-38 seaplane he is trying to sell to the Hochschilds, the first plane ever to land on Eagle Lake. There, waiting on the dock amid a small crowd of family, friends, and laconic men with lumberjacks' checked shirts and twangy upstate accents who work on the property, is the quiet, demure, dark-haired woman he will marry.

Flying north, Boris's seaplane follows the Hudson River up from New York. Five thousand feet into the sky it is easy to forget that the Depression is ravaging the cities below, giving birth to soup kitchens, bread lines, Hoovervilles. Beyond Albany, the Adirondacks begin, and the plane flies for half an hour or more over wilderness, a luxuriantly thick green carpet of forest thrown over the mountains. Boris skirts cottonball clouds that brilliantly reflect the sunlight and bumps through updrafts of wind deflected aloft by the slopes. The woods are interspersed with the shimmer of lakes; the dark of evergreen groves sometimes changes to the lighter white-green of birch—the first growth after a forest fire. Here and there the carpet of trees rises up to bare, rocky mountaintops, some with fire watchtowers or a few picnicking hikers who look up, shade their eyes with their hands, and wave at the plane. Finally Boris passes over the last ridge, and sees beyond it a chain of lakes. On one, three miles from the nearest town, Boris glimpses a small beach, a few fields, and some houses nestled in the woods a short distance back from the water, a little enclave amid endless miles of state forest.

As the plane banks now, the lake outside the window appears to tilt sharply up. Then treetops flash by at eye level, and a sudden sheet of spray shoots up as Boris touches down on the water. The plane approaches a large dock next to a boathouse. This is home for sailboats, canoes, rowboats, and a sleek, powerful Chris-Craft inboard that can carry a dozen people. Now come greetings, introductions, eager hands tying up the plane at the dock. Boris looks around and wonders if the clock has not rolled back twenty years, and he is in the lake and forest country north of St. Petersburg. Then a hand takes his bag, and the group of people stroll up a hundred yards of gently sloping lawn to an imposing three-story building referred to as "the Club House."

Someone hastens to explain to Boris that when Berthold Hochschild and several friends jointly bought this property a quarter of a century earlier, it was a country club that had gone bankrupt. Like any first-time visitor here, Boris notices that the Club House wears its grandeur not lavishly but solemnly: wide eaves overhang a porch the entire length of the building's sunny side, darkening the interior and giving the house a certain heavy look, as if it wears a perpetual frown. This is the building where guests stay, and where the extended family eats its meals. Father sleeps in his own smaller, dark-browed wooden house some distance away, known as the Cottage. A decade later it will be softened and transformed by my mother, filled with cloth weavings, flowers, sweet-smelling balsam pillows, and bright red and yellow Hudson's Bay Company wool blankets.

The Club House has a porch and hearth of rough-cut stone, but almost everything else is wood: dark-stained in the giant living room, lighter knotty pine in the nine guest rooms. A half-dozen maids' rooms and a separate sitting room for their occupants fill a back wing. A myriad of corridors and passageways wind around the two upstairs floors, past a door with a sign, EMPLOYEES ONLY, past an elevator that works with a rope pulley, and past crannies and crawl spaces that would promise a child infinite games of hide-and-seek.

Boris takes a swim, and then explores the property more thoroughly. He sees that it has more docks and houses, a stable and miles of riding trails through the woods, a tennis court, homes for several of the people who work here, and a chicken house which furnishes meat and eggs for the table (during winters in New York, when I was a boy, we still ate Eagle Nest eggs, mailed to us weekly in a battered tin box). The servants call Father "Mr. Harold" and his brother "Mr. Walter"; ten years later, when she is here too, they will call my mother "Mrs. Harold."

Descending the staircase to dinner on his first evening, Boris notes how informally this rather formal family and their guests are dressed: sweaters, more lumberjack shirts, barefoot children. Similarly, this whole property is never referred to as an estate but as a "place" ("Come visit us at our place in the mountains") or as a "camp." Yet the living room is as large as a hotel lobby. Strange, he thinks: the gentry in this new land are different from the same class in Russia; it's almost as if they are pretending they are not landowners at all.

Boris joins the other guests for a before-dinner drink, seating himself near the hearth on a long, curving couch which holds a dozen people. He notices a few objects—a piece of Chinese ivory here, a painting there—that suggest hidden connections to other parts of the world. As the years go by, more and more of these will be from Africa: a wooden head from Nigeria, landscape paintings from Kenya, a zebra skin draped across the piano. Present through all these years are copies of *The London Illustrated News,* full of sepia photographs of military parades and royal weddings, a reminder of the country through which Father's routes to other parts of the world usually lay, and through which, via the London metal markets, The Company's profits flowed homeward.

Twenty years after Boris's arrival in 1930, the country had passed through an economic crisis and a world war, but the Eagle Nest I woke up to on the sunny summer mornings of my childhood was much the same.

I lay in bed long after I woke each morning. My room in the Cottage lay directly below my parents'. In the morning I listened for them: my mother's gentle step, Father's heavier shuffle. If I heard hers but not his, I was relieved, overjoyed; that meant he was still in New York for his three- or four-day summer work week, and had not arrived during the night; I would have her to myself again for the day, one precious day more.

If he was still away, breakfast would be long and relaxed, just she and I. In the morning we might go somewhere together: a short climb or a canoe ride on the lake, before the sun had burned away the water's magical woolly coating of early-morning mist. My mother, with her attention totally on me, was interested in all I said. It didn't even matter if it was a rainy day: then we would light a fire and talk by the hour, or she would read to me. Such days were golden; I wished they would last forever.

If Father was there, I would slip off alone after breakfast, feeling the varying textures of grass and leaves and moss under my bare feet. I would go to hideouts in the woods—a rock or clearing or overgrown fallen tree invested with secret significance. Or to the icehouse, a building at the edge of the forest where, until I was seven or eight, two-hundred-pound blocks of ice that had been cut from the lake in winter were stored for the summer months. They supplied the cooler of one house on the property which didn't have a refrigerator. The ice was kept from melting by an insulating layer of sawdust several feet thick. I rolled and played in the deliciously cool sawdust on hot summer days.

Or I would go to inspect or play with the latest item of

curiosity—a bicycle built for two; a tracked vehicle called a Weasel, which you could drive across streams and fields; a giant kite that took water-skiers into the air when towed behind a boat. All these things appeared for a summer or two and then were put away and replaced with something new. Or I would head out in a rowboat, across the lake to a mossy spot atop a rock where I could relax with a book, quietly hoping to be found by some-one, an aunt or uncle or guest canoeing by, who would—unlike Father, who thought I ought to mix more with other children—praise me for being a boy who read so much.

Sometimes in these wanderings I stopped to talk to one of the men who worked on the grounds. They came from the village nearby: they knew how to skin a deer, build a house, repair a chain saw. In the winter they or others like them worked with lumber contractors who cut trees in our woods and used big draft horses, great statues of muscle, to haul the logs across the frozen lake to the highway. Erwin Hanna, who was superintendent of Eagle Nest for many years, had also been the captain of a steamboat that plied the lakes in the days before the highway was built. Albert Blanchard, who succeeded him, knew all the woodsman's skills and had taught him-self to rebuild small airplanes as well. I envied these men immensely; they and Boris were among the few people I knew who had skills they could do with their hands.

On all these explorations, however, until I was nine, a governess hovered not far away from me, her job to make sure I did not drown in the lake or otherwise come to harm. And (I discovered only years later) to steer me away from the stable, where some of the older boys and girls who were around Eagle Nest in the summer, bolder and less chaperoned than I, put the privacy of the hayloft to good use.

My own playmates were usually imported, carefully selected by my mother: children of her friends or school classmates of mine, whom she invited for a few weeks' visit. At other times I played with the sons, my age, of two men who worked on the property. This was fine until I was ten or eleven, when I began to notice that they always automatically agreed to everything I wanted to do. The puberty of class awareness comes earlier than the puberty of the body. It was a barrier that made us all uneasy, and gradually we ceased spending time together.

My closest playmate throughout those years was my dog, Rex, a friendly, mischievous Labrador with golden fur. I loved him beyond all measure. Loyal and good-spirited, he followed me everywhere, crawling muddy and happy into my tent on camping trips, tracking me down in the woods by scent, swimming after me if I rowed a boat across the lake and had the effrontery to leave him behind.

Rex wagged his tail when Boris talked to him in Russian; he wagged his tail when small children tried to ride him; he wagged his tail when Father sternly tried to punish him for sneaking into the kitchen and stealing a stuffed chicken off the table. "That dog just has to *learn*," Father said, shaking his head in vexed disapproval. My mother sent orders everywhere that Rex was not to be fed anything except his regular afternoon meal. But Rex made friends with kindhearted cooks in all the other houses on the property. Each morning he disappeared for an hour or two, and then walked slowly home to lie in the sun, burping contentedly. For him, too, Eagle Nest was a place of abundance.

On the weekends, when the house was full of guests, there was always waterskiing before lunch. Waterskiing was part of the weekend ritual: all houseguests were expected to appear, at least to cheer from the dock. Father drove the large Chris-Craft motorboat; from the stern, William Hanley, our chauffeur-butler-valet, tossed out the tow rope to skiers. Guests and family took their turns skiing in strict order of precedence: I got a purse-lipped frown from Father if I did not go last.

Then my mother or Gertrude rang an old ship's bell to summon the guests to lunch. Eagle Nest was familiar territory and I was seldom alone with Father here, so I was immune from the nausea attacks which I had elsewhere. Our food, thanks to the cook Boris had hired, was largely Russian. My favorite dish was a wonderful broth with *pelmeni,* Siberian dumplings filled with seasoned chopped meat. Boris, who cheerfully claimed that everything important had been invented by Russians, described *pelmeni*'s history:

"See, you make a big pot of *pelmeni.* Then you put them in a sack on the back of your sleigh. You set off across the steppe. They freeze. You stop for dinner and take out as many *pelmeni* as you want. You put them in boiling water, and there you have it, the world's first frozen food!"

Boris also claimed *pelmeni* as the ancestor of wonton, ravioli, and other inferior imitations: "The Chinese, the Italians, they all got the idea from us in Russia!"

The Russian kitchen also produced *piroshki* (whose name derives from *pir,* a feast)—not the deep-fried soggy monstrosities sold in American delicatessens, but tiny, golden-baked, flaky-crusted pastries stuffed with deli-

cately herbed meat and chopped hard-boiled egg. There
was *borscht,* of course, and *kasha,* and stuffed cabbage
leaves, and a cold creamy soup called *okroshka.* For des-
sert there was a foot-long sliced chocolate roll, thick as
uncut bologna, which, unlike paltry American desserts,
was almost entirely chocolate frosting, the cake part of
it a mere thin spiral inside.

Once a year, on the birthday of Boris and Gertrude's
daughter, Kira, we had charcoal-broiled *shashlik,* mari-
nated lamb shish kebab which took days to prepare. Boris's co-pilot and any other strong young men around
were temporarily drafted into the kitchen to help cut up
what must have been (for there were often several dozen
people at dinner that night) an entire lamb. These birthday feasts for Kira lasted far into the night, long after she
and Gertrude had gone to bed, with much singing and
toasting, to chants of *"Pey-do-dna!* [Drink to the bottom!] *Pey-do-dna!"* accelerating like a train as the person drinking reached the bottom of the glass:
*"Peydodna, peydodna, peydodna, peydodnapeydodna-
peydodnapeydodna!"*

The rest of the time, meals were more sedate. If the day
was warm, lunch at the Club House was out-of-doors, on
a screened veranda that commanded a view of lawn and
trees and lake. Boris sat at one end of the table, Father
at the other, with wives, children, and guests mingled in
between. I tried to sit near Gertrude, who always took a
quiet, sympathetic interest in me, her dark, thoughtful
eyes and slight nods implying that what was important
in my ten-year-old's world mattered to her also. Unlike
my mother, though, Gertrude confided little about herself or her own feelings. Perhaps that would come later,

when I was older, I thought. Surely she would have much to say. After all, had she not, by marrying Boris, made the most daring leap of anyone in the family?

Midway into lunch came a bizarre and, to me, embarrassing ritual. It was called Getting The Beer. I always hoped he would forget, but just as the maids were clearing away the soup bowls, Father would say: "Adam, would you get the beer?"

We always had German dark beer, something which came to be sold widely in the United States later but which was unusual, a conversation piece, in the years right after World War II. It was my job to go around the table and take orders from the guests. "Dark beer or light?" Then I went out to the pantry, opened the bottles, filled the beer mugs, and brought them back to the table. The curious thing about this, of course, is that we had a kitchen staff: the Russian cook and her assistant, and several other women from nearby towns. And, indeed, when I went out into the kitchen, the bottles of dark and light beer were already set out on the counter for me, with the mugs and bottle-opener neatly lined up beside them. I filled the mugs while the maids watched, one or two of the newer ones politely puzzled, the older ones acclimated enough to know that they ought to say, preferably within Father's earshot: "Isn't it nice the way Adam always gets the beer!"

After I handed the beer to people at the table, I sat down again, feeling humiliated, although that, too, had become so habitual that I accepted it as part of the routine. Looking back at it now, I think that feeling came not from having to do a menial task—for I hated having house servants and, later, once I moved away from home, took pride in cooking and cleaning for myself—but rather from the fact that Getting The Beer was a ritual denial that we *were* employers of servants. Getting The Beer was a symbolic representation of the role of a normal host, who prepares the food with his own hands for a more humble table. And I resented particularly that it fell to *me* to make this pretense for Father by proxy.

The custom of Getting The Beer was to persist long after I stopped spending summers at Eagle Nest. When I was older I would come back for a visit of a week or so each year with my wife and children. I noticed that at those weekend lunches some younger guest, by this time the son or even grandson (it had to be a male; that was a ritual within a ritual, symbolically denying that it was women who cooked and waited on table) of one of Father's old friends, someone who was an Eagle Nest regular and knew the routines, would himself, unbidden, take on the role of Getting The Beer.

Afternoon. The glinting of sunlight off the rippled surface of the lake. The silvery shimmer of an aspen in the breeze. The soughing of wind through the grove of pines between the Club House and the Cottage. The softness of Rex's golden fur, still damp from a swim in the lake, as he lay curled up beside me. And, as I sat on a porch chair or under a tree, the smell of British books. Books published in England then smelled different: a faintly briny smell, as if they used seawater in making the paper. For years various British friends of Father's sent me children's books for Christmas.

Many of these were in a series I read endlessly, about Major James Bigglesworth of the Royal Air Force, known as Biggles. For Biggles, World War II was a long, long war indeed, some thirty or forty volumes' worth. He fought in every battle on every front, from Burma to

North Africa to France to secret missions behind the lines. In the midst of aerial dogfights Biggles always "smiled grimly" or "smiled faintly" or "gave a tight-lipped smile." As bullets whizzed through his cockpit windshield he exclaimed, "My gosh!" or "What a ghastly show!" On those long Eagle Nest afternoons Biggles shot Nazis out of the sky, always finding in the opposing German squadron his archenemy, Erich von Stalhein, a sadistic Prussian aristocrat with a monocle. But, on the last page of each book, as von Stalhein's smoking Messerschmitt plummeted toward earth, out popped a parachute, so you knew he would live to fight again.

I lived almost totally in books. As I approached adolescence, it seemed to be in the realm of books, rather than in the real world, that I was aware of the first unexpected flickers of sexuality. Suddenly I noticed a new dimension in all those World War II adventure books. In one, a Norwegian woman was the mistress of a Nazi officer, passing his secrets on to the Underground. I've long forgotten the volume's title, but still remember a sentence from it: "And at night, he could do anything he wanted with her long, white body." For months I turned the words around in my head.

With a secret intensity, I also read the *Reader's Digest,* which my mother subscribed to. Then, as now, the *Digest* was very big on two themes: anti-Communism and premarital chastity. Never did it wax more fervent than in combining the two. I remember one article about the alarming rise of sexual immorality under Communism. Wild parties in Czechoslovakia; debauchery in the dark depths of Polish coal mines; orgiastic summer camps for Bulgarian teenagers. I read and reread this piece dozens of times, and remember phrases still. So many nights of delicious fantasies: did the *Digest*'s editors know what they had wrought?

Everything at Eagle Nest happened according to a set schedule, which Father announced to his guests, clinking a knife on his wineglass for silence, at the end of the first meal of the weekend: waterskiing at 12, sherry at 1, lunch at 1:15, riding at 3:30, and so on. Finally, at 6:15 each evening, Father swam across the lake and back. He swam by a never-changing routine, stepping into the water instead of diving, shifting from breaststroke to sidestroke to backstroke to crawl at regular intervals. As a safety precaution, someone followed in an electric-powered boat, cruising noiselessly some yards behind him, ready— though almost never having to do so—to help him out of the water in case of cramps or a sudden thunderstorm. I went along for the ride. It was the time of day when the lake was at its loveliest, its surface a calm, dark mirror for the mountains. Sounds echoed across it: the splash of his hands in the water, a murmur of voices and laughter on shore; the wind had quieted; all was at peace. Father was in the water, so I could not talk to him, but I could still be close to him, fulfilling some obligation and perhaps, after all, some wish.

Dinner was segregated. The children and their entourage ate early, the grown-ups later. So dinner was: me; my governess of the moment; Boris and Gertrude's daughter, Kira; her Russian governess, Mrs. Gretchina; and whatever other children were visiting. Of these there were usually many: cousins, children of weekend guests, the children of Kira's Russian gymnastics teacher. Most of the talk at the children's table was in Russian, which frustrated me. We finished as the grown-ups began having cocktails. A few minutes later, it was time for me to make the rounds of the circle of sofas and chairs and say goodnight to everyone, always a bit uncertain just whom to shake hands with, whom to kiss. If Father wore a suit and tie, my heart leapt; it meant he was leaving for New York after dinner, on the overnight train. My mother would be mine again.

Bed. The time seemed endless, suspended between waking and sleep, between water and sky. Sometimes a guest played the piano, and from my bed I could hear the music echoing out across the smooth surface of the lake. Occasionally, if I woke later in the evening, I could hear the splashing and laughter and voices from the dock which meant that some of the younger guests were taking a furtive late-night nude swim—something out of the question during the day. Those sounds, too, merged in my mind with that of the music on the water; they seemed an image of promise, of yearning, of the existence of some beauty and fulfillment in life that was denied me. It was as if all year I had waited to come here for the summer; all day I had held my breath waiting for some magic moment, and now I saw only its sign; the secret remained as locked away as ever.

As I drifted to sleep there came the sound of a solitary outboard motorboat, going slowly through the lake, taking a lone fisherman home at the end of the day. Perhaps he looked up as he passed, and wondered what went on in the dark-browed houses among the trees. Then the hollow cry of a loon, the loneliest of all birds. And the calls of half a dozen other birds, whose names I did not know but whose sounds I will remember until the day I die. And just as the day ended, so did the week, with Father going, and the summer, with all of us leaving Eagle

Nest, and finally those summers themselves were no more; their character gradually changed, and the exact moment that happened cannot be pinpointed, any more than you can mark the exact moment you fall asleep.

VII

All through my childhood, people would say, "Your father? Oh, of course, what a wonderful man. I know him well." But our language is deficient. There should be two words, one for knowing a person as a friend or colleague, the other for knowing someone as a parent. I never felt that way about my mother. For her, one word would do. But Father was different. Others seemed only to see a man of wit, learning, and great integrity, someone who generously bestowed gifts and invitations on his wide circle of friends, a world traveler who spoke five languages, a businessman of unusual liberalism, and a self-taught expert on Adirondack history: in his spare time, he wrote a prize-winning book on the subject, and founded a fine museum. A somewhat uncomfortable man, true; shy, a bit distant, sometimes ill at ease, but still, how lucky you must be to have had him as a father! And besides, Adam, you had everything: houses, chauffeurs, maids, money—the whole world was yours. How can you complain?

All this was true. But there was another side to Father, whose weight only I seemed to feel. Where I most experienced it, even amid all the pleasures of Eagle Nest, was in the recurring outbursts of his intense disapproval. These did not come daily, perhaps not even weekly. But they affected me so powerfully that they colored the time between them as well.

Like bouts of a disease, these episodes always followed a set pattern. First was my crime itself. To begin with, Father disapproved of some of my hobbies, tentative as they were, thinking them frivolous. I used to listen to an old shortwave radio that had been *his,* even, which I found discarded in the attic and fixed up—until one day he solemnly said he thought I was spending too much time on this. Or sometimes my wrongdoing involved my being, in his eyes, too uncommunicative and not polite enough with a guest. Or it was the sin of not being grateful enough for something—not thanking someone with enough enthusiasm, say, for a present I really didn't want. But there was a treacherously narrow path between being not animated enough and being too much so. For, most often of all, my crime would be that of taking too much space, of talking too much: at the table, in a carload of family and guests en route to Eagle Nest, anywhere he and I were together with other people.

It was so easy to slip into this pattern, particularly if I had been spending time with my mother: to her I was a precocious, entertaining child; she was endlessly delighted by my thoughts and questions and fantasies. When I was with her, there was no such thing as talking too much. I could chatter for hours and she loved it. But when Father and a group of his friends were there, I was surrounded by an invisible trip wire. I could never figure out in advance just where it lay, until suddenly I knew, with a sinking-stomach despair, that I had inadvertently stumbled against it. I would be talking and giggling, happily taking center stage, when I would see the moment at which Father found me guilty: a slight pursing of the lips, a raising of one eyebrow, a cryptic word or two which I knew would be expanded on later: "Adam! I think that's enough for now."

At this point some valve opened inside me, and I felt a pervasive dread traveling through my whole body as if I had taken some powerful, swift-acting drug. Sometimes I tried desperately to win back his approval by being very affectionate, but it never worked.

The next stage, a few hours later, was confirmation of the verdict. Often I overheard my parents talking, when they thought I was asleep, or when I hid behind a tree as they walked from the Club House to the Cottage. Always Father would bring up the subject:

"I thought Adam was talking too much at the table today."

"Yes, you're probably right, Harold," my mother would agree. She never reprimanded me herself and never seemed angry with me. But she always agreed with him.

"I think I better speak to him about it," Father said.

"Yes, dear."

I went to sleep subdued. When I woke the next morning, it seemed like a normal day until, a few moments after opening my eyes, I remembered. In the morning would come the announcement. He would say: "Adam, can I see you in my study at two o'clock, please?" Or perhaps he would be upstairs working, and my mother would be the messenger. "Father wants to see you at two o'clock. O.K., dear?"

The morning was long. I could not concentrate when I read. I was cloaked in dread.

Two o'clock. I waited until maybe 2:03, but to wait any longer would risk the additional crime of being late, something guaranteed at any time to make Father upset. I knocked on his door.

"Come in!"

"Hi . . . you wanted . . . to talk . . . to me?"

"Sit down, Adam. I'll be with you in a moment."

A shuffle of papers; a signature on a document; at last Father put the work on his desk aside, and leaned back in his chair.

"I've been meaning to talk to you, Adam, about something that happened yesterday. I thought it was quite rude when you were talking so much at the table last night. Couldn't you see it was preventing people from having their own conversation?"

It didn't last long. No spanking. No beating. No raised voice. Maybe just two or three minutes of talk. Father's words were always carefully chosen, balanced, never casual, as if each phrase had been inspected and been found irrefutable before he permitted it to exit his lips.

I couldn't bring myself to look at him. I craved for an earthquake to bring the session to an end. What made it so much worse was that Father was always, it seemed, fully reasonable. He spoke in a voice which carried in it the full weight of his authority, of his wide reputation for morality, a voice whose very quietness contained the expectation of unquestioning obedience.

After he had finished whatever he had to say—all of which I had known was coming for perhaps a full twenty-four hours—Father would pause for me to respond. He listened, it might be said, in a distinct tone of voice: his right hand, leathery, mottled, crept up to his face to support his chin with its thumb, while first and second fingers bracketed his mouth, as if holding in his own speech while he heard me out. In a way this was the most frightening moment of all, this careful, alert listening from someone whose entire bearing and role in life was that of a man who expected to be listened *to*. Of course I never really dared argue; his evidence always seemed convincing.

At last, to put the seal on the encounter, Father would say, in words which ostensibly dissipated, but in fact thickened, the cloud that hung over me:

"All right? I think you now see what I mean. I won't speak about this incident again."

Then he motioned for me to come around behind his desk so we could exchange kisses on the cheek, that gesture between us in which there was always an element of submission: now it was a sign that I had acknowledged my error and would reform. Our session was over.

The impact of one of these reprimands echoed in my head for days afterward. Take one such incident; multiply it by a hundred. Add to the picture the fact that I had no brothers or sisters, no allies, no witnesses for the defense. Why did this process seem all the worse for his never raising his voice, never striking me? I think because I therefore had no chance to get angry *back;* I never doubted that he was merciful and that I was guilty.

My tendency automatically to assume my own guilt spread from those sessions in Father's study over the rest of my life.

Once, when I was in seventh grade, my history teacher gave me a book to read and report on to the class—a book about the battles of the Civil War. I still remember it: the cover was blue, with crossed swords and a soldier's cap. A few days after he gave it to me, I lost the book. I felt complete panic.

"What happened to that special report you were going to give us, Hochschild?"

"I'm . . . working on it, sir."

Desperately, I searched everywhere: desk, locker, odd corners of the classroom, my room at home. No book.

Days went by. I avoided eye contact with the teacher and slipped out of class as soon as the bell rang so I would never find myself alone with him. At one level of awareness, I knew he was an absentminded man and might well have forgotten about the book. But I still lived in fear that he would remember.

I searched again and again. The school year ended. The summer was an idyll of Europe and Eagle Nest, but every few days I would remember the lost book, wince, and feel my day darken.

Then, one day in the fall, I was studying in the school library. I looked up for a moment, and there, on a shelf at my eye level, was the missing book, crossed swords and all. It had been a library book, and somebody must have seen it lying about and simply returned it. This was the one place I had never thought to look. A vast rush of relief swept through me; I could see the sky again.

VIII

When I think today of those encounters with Father, and still more when I dream of them, they are always at Eagle Nest. But most of the time we were elsewhere.

I was born in New York; we lived there during the school year when I was small, lived there because one didn't live anywhere else. People did, I supposed from looking at a map, but why? New York was the capital of the world. The exact center of New York, the capital of the capital, was approximately Fifth Avenue and Fifty-eighth Street: here were the carriages that took you for rides in Central Park, steamy breath puffing out of the horses' nostrils as they waited for customers on winter days; the delicious burning-charcoal smell from the little carts that sold roast chestnuts and hot pretzels; F. A. O. Schwarz, the giant toy store with its tempting paradise of electric trains. Close by was the Central Park Zoo, where my mother took me almost every day; the Sherry Netherland Hotel, where my uncle and aunt had an apartment; and our own apartment high above Park Avenue only two blocks away. So: a New York of fur-coated ladies waiting under awnings for taxis, of doormen who touched their caps to you, a New York which had no streets, really, only apartments of family and friends, doctors' offices, my school. I rarely went anywhere else, and was always whisked from one familiar place to another behind the rolled-up windows of a taxi or a limousine.

For my mother and thus for me, there was something vaguely menacing about New York. Its streets were full of cars that might run over you, germs that might give you diseases, "juvenile delinquents" who might attack you. I was not allowed to cross streets on my own; if I went out without my governess, I could go no farther than the toy store on our own block.

New York was Father's world, a world he would someday push me into, and that is what made me not like it. That world was harsh, competitive, a man's world without the comforting presence of my mother. Sometimes Father took me to box at his club, where the walls were covered with nineteenth-century lithographs of bare-knuckled fighters and faded sepia photographs of the Yale boxing teams of 1898 or 1901. I never liked the boxing, but didn't mind doing it with him too much, since he knew not to hit me hard. But occasionally I was with a friend; he would put gloves on the two of us and have us box each other; I would end up frightened and in tears.

We lived on the twenty-first floor, not above the noise of the city, but at its topmost layer. Lying awake at night I heard the roar of buses starting up at intersections, cabs honking, sirens, a shrill far-off policeman's whistle, the more hornlike whistles doormen used to call cabs: blurring together it all seemed the voice of a world I would be lost in, where that sudden nausea might attack me at any moment. The street noise was like a warning note coming at me down a dark tunnel whose end was the end of childhood, which seemed to me a kind of death. Hearing once that some animal had escaped from the Bronx Zoo, I dreamt that lions had escaped from our zoo, right next door in Central Park, and were climbing up the outside of the building to get me. I woke screaming; my mother comforted me. I knew that as long as she lived, the lions would never get me. But after that?

When I turned eight, we moved, at my mother's urging, to Princeton, New Jersey. If New York was Father's, Princeton was hers. She wanted trees, grass, a garden, space for me to have Rex and for her to build a stately house with a courtyard. And I think they both hoped that in a more suburban setting I might overcome the paralyzing succession of phobias I had had ever since the mastoid operation a few years before.

Father took the commuter train to Manhattan each day. My parents ate dinner after he got home, so I had my meal earlier, on a tray a maid brought to my room. She had a voice that would pierce stone walls; after she came back to take the tray away, I could hear her, through several intervening doors, reporting to my mother: "MRS. HOCHSCHILD, HE FINISHED THE CHICKEN AND THE POTATO, BUT NOT THE CARROTS."

After dinner, I went in the limousine to meet Father's train. I liked the drive to the station. I sat in the front seat with William Hanley, our British-born chauffeur, who had driven for The Company in London. From him I got a corporal's-eye view of Montgomery's strategy at El Alamein, an introduction to understanding the relative prestige of the different regiments of the Guards, some of the basics of repairing and operating a tank, and a great deal about the Royal Family.

I liked the trip home from the station even more. For some reason—perhaps he was grateful that I had come to meet him—the short drive back to the house with Father was pleasant. I was always safe from his reprimands then. He asked about my day at school and told me about people he had seen during the day in New York. In contrast to my usual wariness of the sudden outbursts of his disapproval, I knew this was a curious daily interlude of safety. Why couldn't things have been that way always?

My mother had picked Princeton to move to because she had grown up there: her mother had been the *grande dame* of the town, its premier hostess, landowner, and doer of good civic deeds. That first year my mother reestablished the links from her youth. I played on the floor and listened as she called people to assemble guests for dinner parties, saying, "Hello, this is Mary Mar*quand* Hochschild," with that slight emphasis on the middle name.

There was a collegiate Princeton and a black Princeton, but the Princeton we lived in was an expanse of rambling clapboard houses and wide, shady streets that rustled with windblown leaves in the fall. Its inhabitants were often from the old families my mother had grown up with: many of the men were Princeton graduates who had lived their youth, college years, and adulthood here in the same town. On autumn Saturdays everybody went to the football game in Palmer Stadium; when Princeton scored a touchdown, I could hear the cheering from our house, clear on the other side of town. Periodically, like a figure from another century, along the sidewalks of our little world of station wagons and patios and oak-shaded lawns would walk an old man with a thick shock of white hair, a large-eyed, luminous smile, and no socks. It was Albert Einstein, who lived two blocks away.

Our house had a staff of five or so. How many euphemisms there are for servants! "Staff." "Help." "Someone"—as in "Do you have someone for your kitchen this summer?" Or even just a possessive pronoun and first name, as in "Do you still have your marvelous Ellen?"

Our marvelous Ellen. She was a kind, gentle woman from Ireland. She had left an impoverished farm there as a teenager, married in the New World, then seen her husband die young. She laughed with disbelief when I told her solemnly that I had decided to have no servants when I grew up. "But Adam dear, who's going to cook?" She worked for us until she died, in her sixties, and she had worked for my mother before my parents married—eternally, deeply grateful that my mother had given her a job in the depths of the Depression. She, a young widow with three small children to support, cooking and cleaning for a single woman her own age. Who had taken care of Ellen's children, it occurs to me now, while she was cooking my mother's dinners? I never thought to ask her. Grateful to be given a job. It took me a long time to see all the assumptions those words contained.

For my mother, moving to Princeton was coming home; for Father it was a further step into that world he so much wanted to be part of, for Princeton was thoroughly WASP. Childhood friends of my mother's a few blocks away from us lived in an attractive stone house that had sheltered some of General Washington's troops. The ivied walls of the homes where my parents went to black-tie dinner parties housed few Jews. My life up to this point had been solid Christmas trees and Santa Claus, plus nightly prayers with my governess, who was extremely devout. Added onto this, in Princeton, was Sunday school in the Episcopal church that served the fashionable end of town. I hated it. It was Father who seemed most intent that I should go—even though neither of my parents was a churchgoer. My mother finally let me stop when she met the minister and saw how sanctimonious he was.

As another part of the assimilation process, I was sent to a dancing class. We had to wear white gloves, and were taught by a dapper instructor with shining black shoes, who arrived weekly from New York. Each session began with the white-gloved boys, at a signal, dashing across the ballroom floor in a flying charge, elbowing each other out of the way, to choose partners from the white-gloved girls lined up against the opposite wall. The first day I clumsily navigated my way around the floor with one girl all afternoon, too tongue-tied to ask her name.

Like the sons of all the people my parents knew, I was sent to the private boys' school in town, Princeton Country Day. The headmaster admired traditional English boarding schools; the Latin teacher's idea of homework was to have you copy passages from the grammar book many times over; another teacher pinched the bottoms of boys he liked. The desks were bolted to the floor and even the nine-year-olds had to wear coats and ties. The boys called the teachers "Sir." The word even became a name at times, as in "Sir asked me to do this." Our hockey coach once fell on the ice and cracked his skull (not quite thoroughly enough, some of us felt); while he was recuperating, my class was told to send him get-well cards. He acknowledged mine with a card of his own, signed, "Affectionately, 'Sir.' "

In Princeton I was always painfully aware of being different, even from the other boys at our end of town. Part of it was that my parents were nearly a generation older than everyone else's. "Is that your father or your grandfather?" If Father showed up at a school baseball game,

the other boys and even their parents seemed more subdued and on their best behavior. I felt conspicuous for
calling him by such a formal name as "Father." I was also
embarrassed by how extravagantly we lived. When we
were practicing numbers in French class, the teacher
went around the room asking each boy, *"Combien de
chambres y-a-t-il dans votre maison?"* When my turn
came, a wave of laughter swept the class.

I began to dread rides in the family limousine, a long
black Chrysler. When William Hanley took me to school
in it, I slid far down in the front seat, trying to stay out
of the view of the group of my classmates who bicycled
to school each day along the same route. I timidly tried
to talk to Father about this. He listened solemnly—he always heard me out, never interrupted anybody. But
when I was finished he declared, "Well, Adam, I just
don't think having a car like that is anything to be
ashamed of."

My mother seemed to understand how I felt. But, having heard Father's statement of opinion, she was unwill-
ing to contest it. Eventually I got William to drop me off
several blocks from school, where no one could see me.

For my mother, I could do no wrong. But when Father
had spoken his mind on an issue, she deferred to him.
Many years later in Los Angeles I met a childhood playmate from Princeton. "She softened you up for him," he
said.

She was sensitive enough to know that there was
something wrong between her husband and her son, but
she dared not look too closely. She almost seemed to
hope that if she could just act as if Father and I were the
best of friends, sooner or later we would be.

One Sunday in Princeton my mother was reading aloud something from a newspaper supplement when she and I were at breakfast alone. It was a quiz on "How Well Do You Know Your Child?" She was trying to answer it, question by question.

One item was: "Who is his greatest hero?"

She answered immediately: "Oh, your father, of course," and moved quickly on to the next question.

Home movies that jerkily pan across those years show a spindly, uncomfortable-looking boy, sometimes grinning nervously, always dressed properly for the event being photographed—a one-piece snowsuit for winter; boots, jodhpurs, and leather gloves for horseback riding—when another boy might have worn blue jeans on both occasions. The child whose image flickers on the screen is almost always with a governess, seldom with friends.

My mother went to great lengths to make our home a center of children's activities: arranging for my governess to be a Cub Scout den mother, arranging for soccer and softball games to take place on our lawn. When I had a birthday party not long after we moved to Princeton, it was she, not I, who figured out which boys to invite. The party went well nonetheless, but at the height of the festivity, when the other boys and I were laughing and eating cake and clowning in pointed paper hats, I looked up and saw my parents together in the doorway, smiling at the scene. I felt I could read in their smiles satisfaction, love, but also relief: we pulled it off, avoided a disaster; maybe he'll make it after all.

But to me it seemed I would not. I felt immensely more solemn than other boys. I was timid about going to their homes, especially for meals. And if I was invited somewhere for a weekend, or for dinner, without my parents, I often panicked and got sick at the last moment. Father would be exasperated, my mother comforting.

Best of all, I loved staying home sick, when she would take care of me, read aloud to me, bring me glasses of ginger ale in bed. That drab cold world of school, where I always felt on the sidelines, receded; in *her* world I was the center. As I grew older, I became disturbingly healthy, but grew skilled at exaggerating small symptoms.

What few friends I had seemed not only arranged but purchased. I had only two regular playmates, both of whom were showered with favors by my parents: invitations to Eagle Nest summer and winter, trips to Europe and elsewhere with us. They put up with my shyness and lack of interest in sports. By the time I was twelve or thirteen, I began to sense that they kept playing with me only because their families must have insisted: " . . . the Hochschilds have done so much for you."

It was one of these boys whom I met again years later in Los Angeles, one evening in an apartment high above a crisscross of freeways, a glass cabin in the sky. We talked about the time he had been our guest on a trip to the Caribbean: I remembered that he had ended up playing mostly with other teenagers on the ship, finding me, no doubt, a stick-in-the-mud. He confirmed this. He said that my parents had seen this happening and had told him:

"It's O.K. for you to spend your evenings with the other kids, as long as you first spend half an hour with Adam every night after dinner."

In the summers we sometimes traveled for a month or so before going to Eagle Nest. These trips seemed managed by the gestures of Father's right hand. Pointing up and out, like Lenin in Soviet statues, to hail a taxi. Making a scribble in the air, to signal for the check at a restaurant. Pointing out and down, in the customs shed of a steamship pier: *there,* those are our bags. A hand with fingers folded over, a five-dollar bill or a pound note or a ten-mark note inside, ready to be pressed into the doorman's hand as we leave the hotel where we've been staying. A hand that had hailed rickshaws in Shanghai, carriages in the Kaiser's Germany, bicycle taxis in Paris during World War II, when there was no gasoline; a hand, like those of merchants in Renaissance paintings, which rested confidently on the globe.

A hand, also, that grasped the room key before he crossed the hotel doorstep, that held the ticket before he got out of the car at the airport, that had the tip ready before the porter put down the bags. Somewhat anxiously, Father was always drawn to the mechanics of travel: finding the best airline flights, the most comfortable hotels, the most recommended excursions—all of which he arranged months in advance.

There were many hotels where we stayed regularly, year after year: Grosvenor House, in London, where The Company had a permanent suite, in which Father had actually lived for some months during World War II, at a time when officers above a certain rank were allowed to find their own accommodations; the floating hotels—the ships of the Cunard Line, where, as in the other places, Father was a regular, was known; the Park Hotel Vitznau, on the Lake of Lucerne, where the concierge knew even more languages than Father; and the Sacher in Vienna, with the doors to its rooms upholstered in red leather, where once in the dining room my mother recognized a Chicago family she knew, with a name one sees on cans of meat, noticing them with such matter-of-factness that I began to grasp that the world is not divided by cities and countries, as they said in school, but in more subtle ways.

Always there were displays put on for our benefit. A boxing tournament among the crew members of a steamship, which passengers could watch. Native dances in Africa. A village of Lapp tents in Norway, erected just where the cruise ship's boats docked. A huge resort hotel in Virginia where all the guests were white and all the waiters black: they carried trays of food on their heads, and once a year had outdoor foot races this way.

Although I lived in Princeton, I did not quite live in the United States. Once, many years later, on a day-long train trip the length of California, I joined a group of travelers in the club car that clustered around someone with a guitar, and we spent several hours singing folk songs. I felt elated at my successful deception: I'm fooling them; they think I'm a native; I'm passing.

And the cruises:

The French Line requests passengers to place money and jewelry in safekeeping at the purser's office on A Deck. Passengers on special diets are invited to make their requirements known to the chief steward. The Cunard Line advises passengers dining ashore to consume bottled beverages only, and to avoid uncooked greens or vegetables. The ship's surgeon has remedies available for digestive discomfort.

"Let's check the passenger list," my mother always says at the beginning of the voyage, "and see who we know."

The deckhands, who appear only briefly, wrestling a

huge hawser into coils after we cast off from the pier, are Oriental: Filipinos? Malays? It is rumored that the engine-room crew are Goans. Or is it turbaned Sikhs? I do not know; they never emerge. On the *Caronia* a wealthy and mysterious Spanish lady speaks to no one, and travels with her own private maid. On the *Kungsholm* there is a man who does nothing but take cruises all year long; with a raised eyebrow Father refers to him as "a cruise bum." At Barbados, St. Thomas, the other islands which blur into one, there are always the black boys, swimming beside the ship, diving for the coins we toss down from the decks.

On this home that encompasses us as we go about the world there is breakfast, midmorning bouillon, lunch, tea, dinner, midnight buffet. The wood of the cabin walls and shelves is finished with a smooth lacquer of high, mirrorlike gloss. At night I sleep soundly, that deep, cradled sleep of being at sea, a sleep touched gently by foghorns, a sleep in itself a journey, like those of other travelers on the ocean: of Father going to war, of Berthold crossing the Atlantic for the first time. Then, waking: a brilliant dawn, the sound of a motor launch puttering toward shore. Where are we? Is this Cape Town? Rio? Mombasa? Bombay?

IX

In the shadow of Father, my childhood landscape often seemed somber. But in contrast, sweeping through it like an elemental life-force, was the figure of Boris. Across the placid summer evenings of Eagle Nest, with their soft Ivy League voices, white-aproned maids, and after-dinner coffee in demitasses, his booming laugh was like the Grumman Mallard's motors warming up. It was as if Tom Jones had landed by accident in a novel by Henry James.

Sometimes Boris did drop from the sky by surprise, if he had not been able to reach us beforehand by phone. A distant hum in the air; others might think it was a plane with a single engine, but I recognized the deeper chord of the Mallard's two. I raced out on the lawn shouting: "There it is! I see him! I see him!" At treetop height, Boris roared over the Club House to announce his arrival, his grinning face visible at the cockpit window. Then everybody piled into cars and motorboats to go down to the hangar on the next lake and meet the plane. Boris was always returning from somewhere exciting: from test-flying captured Nazi jet fighters for the Air Force at the end of World War II; from flying moose hunters to the Canadian North; from landing in a rough sea to pick up films of the *Andrea Doria* shipwreck for CBS. He usually brought with him a planeload of Rus-

sian friends, and the whole pace of Eagle Nest turned fes-
tive as they arrived.

Boris's sturdy, tree-trunk torso exuded strength and
health. He had a superb tenor voice, and, after dinner
when the mood was right, he stood by the piano, fixed
his blue eyes intently on first one, then another woman
among the assembled guests, and sang arias from *La
Belle Helène, La Traviata,* and other operas and oper-
ettas. During one interlude of his extraordinary life,
when he had been stranded for some months in Europe
in the twenties without wars or airplanes, he had sung
professionally. It was with the money he earned as a
singer that he was able to pay his way to the United
States in 1923.

Boris never bragged about his past. Only a decade
after he died was I to discover that, unknown to any of
the Hochschilds, there was a small book about him. It
had been published in Russian by a society of Tsarist war
veterans, a transcription of some interviews Boris gave
about his life. Here is just a taste of that book, one story
never told in the decorous atmosphere of Eagle Nest.

It is August 1914. Germany and Russia have just gone
to war. Boris's infantry regiment is mobilized and ordered to the front. En route it stops for a few days in a
small Ukrainian town. A traveling musical comedy
troupe has been stranded by the outbreak of war in the
same spot: all space in trains has been taken over by the
Army. So the company passes its time by putting on per-
formances for the soldiers. Boris and two fellow officers
attend. The leading actress, according to Boris, "was one
of the most beautiful women I have ever seen in my long
life." All three men are infatuated with her. They draw
lots.

The first officer asks her to dinner after the night's performance, and comes back to the barracks rejected. The following evening the second officer woos her—and also comes home early. Each reports that she has questioned him about Boris. The third night it is Boris's turn. During the day the regiment receives orders to march for the front the next morning at dawn. Of that last night, all we know is what Boris says: "Before going for dinner I packed my few belongings and gave my orderly the order to bring me a pistol and my possessions straight to the place where the battalions were to be assembled at 5 a.m. I had a hope that I would not have to return to the barracks that night. That hope was justified."

Boris had the effect on me that he did partly because I saw him side by side with my parents. Father was always formal; he seldom called anyone, even his own brother, by his or her common nickname. He was uncomfortable with anybody loud or boisterous, people he called "glad-handers" or "Miami Beach types, with palm-tree shirts." Both he and my mother were among the most refined people imaginable. Except for an extremely rare "hell" or "damn," I never heard either of them utter a four-letter word. They were visibly jarred if anyone else did. Once when I was traveling with Father, a mechanical breakdown stranded us in a small airport and we had to wait in a mechanics' shack that was wallpapered from floor to ceiling with *Playboy* photos. He grimaced in embarrassment, saying nothing as the minutes ticked by.

Boris, on the other hand, reveled in earthiness. Once we were sitting in front of the big fireplace at the Club House and he was telling me about some battle he had fought in, during which a bullet had grazed a friend standing next to him, nicking an artery. "And

Ahhhdahhhm, hees *blawwwd* vas awwl awwwver me!"
Boris slapped his riding-booted leg and roared with
laughter. "I vas *rret* from het to foooot!"

Boris loved friends, airplanes, champagne, steak tar-
tare, horses, and, above all, beautiful women. When he
made a much-noted twenty-eight-hour small-plane
crossing of the North Atlantic, a newspaper headline
read: "Sergievsky, Wife, and Ballerina Fly to London
'Just for Fun.' " In a natural, almost animal way, he was
the most masculine man I ever knew. I do not mean that
robust sexuality and physical bravery are the province of
men only, but merely that, having lived the life he had,
Boris had no need for any *macho* pretense. He was at
ease with himself.

Normally gregarious, Boris sometimes fell silent in Father's presence. He usually drove cars at airplane speed,
as if preparing to pull back the wheel and take off at any
moment. Gertrude would be calling out from the back
seat, "Boris! Slow down! Please slow down!" The State
of New York finally took his license away. But if Father
was along, he drove at normal speed, without being
asked.

By the time I was twelve or thirteen I began to notice
that there were times Boris was excluded. Father and his
brother and sister would sometimes have a meeting
about family finances while everyone was at Eagle Nest.
The wives of the two brothers always took part, but Boris
would be off in a corner reading.

Gertrude transferred a good share of her inheritance
to Boris over the years, and Boris became a sort of one-
man Russian-American welfare society, genially dis-
pensing money and presents to needy friends, Russian

churches, favorite dancers. An easy touch, he kept in-
vesting in the business ventures of various friends, from
experimental-aircraft factories to Russian restaurants.
The results were usually disastrous. Father, who had
never really forgiven Boris for marrying his sister, shook
his head and wrote Boris solemn letters of reproach:
You've had a distinguished career as a pilot, Boris, but
really I think that in these fiscal matters you'd be well
advised to be more prudent.

Surprisingly, my mother appreciated Boris greatly. Beneath her fearfulness, her protected upbringing, and her
hypochondria lay a deep curiosity about people. She had
a rare capacity to delight in those far different from herself. Although she never allowed herself to say anything
critical of Father, in her heart she must have known that
Boris brought into the extended family a zest and spirit
it sorely lacked. As I was growing up it was from her, not
from Father or Gertrude, that I first learned most of what
I know about Boris's past.

Whatever his problems as an investor, Boris was a grand
success in friendships. He joined everything, from the
Explorers Club to opera lovers' associations. And he
knew everybody, from Commander Whitehead of the
Schweppes ads to the man who owned the restaurant in
the Eiffel Tower. But his closest friends were all Russians, and the sound of the language flowed through my
summer days like music.

Within a decade of Boris's arrival, most of the staff at
Eagle Nest were Tsarist émigrés. Whenever there was a
vacancy, Boris had a Russian friend who needed a job.
Many were former aristocrats or officers, born to lead

hussars on parade, now growing old in a land of Levit-towns and Doggie Diners. A succession of such men took care of the horses at the stable: Prince Dadiani from Georgia; Captain Ouroumoff, who brewed a sweetish, foul-tasting liqueur out of some tiny wild red berries on the property whose English name no one knew; and—for most of my childhood—Colonel Natirboff, the father of Boris's co-pilot. A tall, dark-haired, onetime cavalry commander and devout Muslim, he came from one of the several hundred families which, he said, once owned all of Circassia, in the northern Caucasus.

Even some of the horses had names like Bogatyr and Djigit. For several summers I and other children had riding lessons from Colonel Kadir Azamat Guirey, another Circassian cavalryman, who was related to Natirboff. Arriving in America as a refugee, he had taught his children to pray in Circassian: *"Ya Allah Bolshevikher worakod!"* (O Allah, may the Bolsheviks perish!) But Allah had not obliged, and Colonel Guirey now ran a riding school in New York. He came to Eagle Nest some weekends, and we galloped and jumped in a wooden-fenced ring while he shouted out commands: "Heelsss *down*! Toes *ooop*! Elbows at ze *sites*! Knees *eeen*! Eyesss looook strrraight between ze earsss of ze *horsssse*!"

One of these aristocratic stable-tenders was fired on the spot by Boris for making some critical remark about how Boris and a young lady visitor kept going for four-hour rides on trails that were two hours long. The woman in question, whom Boris proclaimed to be the daughter of "an old, old friend, a very close friend," came frequently, almost every weekend. Her visits became the subject of much local gossip. There was an unspoken understanding among everyone that Boris's affairs would be tolerated if they took place out of sight, but this was too much. Gertrude suffered quietly, but said nothing, at least in public.

Finally, my mother told me, "Father spoke to him about it."

Boris never invited the woman to Eagle Nest again.

Like the main dining table, the Club House kitchen was also a mix of cultures. Maids and a handyman from the small village a few miles away worked together with the Russian cook and her assistant. The latter, Mrs. Phillipoff, knew little English but spoke excellent French. And underneath her kerchief and apron she had the bearing of an aristocrat. In her youth, it was rumored, she had danced in the famous émigré ballet company, the Ballet Russe de Monte Carlo. Boris and Gertrude reportedly had invited her to Eagle Nest as a guest, and she had said, "If you really want to do me a favor, you can give me a job. I need one."

As a sign that the Sergievskys considered Mrs. Phillipoff their social equal, even though she was washing their dishes, she was always invited to bring her young grandson with her to Eagle Nest for the summer. He was a bright boy of great charm, already trilingual at the age of seven. He swam and played with me and my cousins and the children of guests, and he ate with us at the main table instead of in the kitchen, as if taking by proxy the social status to which his grandmother was entitled.

The Russian party never ended. Boris staged a horse show for the children, and brought a big box of prize ribbons up from New York; there was one for everybody, and he made sure I got the best: a blue ribbon with streamers two feet long. Russians celebrated everything twice, it seemed: birthdays on your birthday and also on the birthday of the saint you were named after; Christmas on Christmas itself and also on Christmas Eve, when other presents were opened.

At Christmas there was a ceiling-high tree in the Club House living room. On it Gertrude hung little silver cones and hollow balls, which she filled with nonpareils—round, bittersweet chocolate wafers studded with white speckles—which we children were allowed to discover on the tree after dinner. On winter days Boris would take their daughter, Kira, for a sleigh ride down to the airplane hangar, urging the horse to a fast trot. Lap robes kept them warm; the horse's breath puffed out in clouds in the cold air. I lay on my sled, which was linked to the back of the sleigh by a long rope. My eyes were closed against the bits of snow and ice tossed rearward by the horse's hooves. Rex raced beside me, his golden fur powdered with snow. The sleigh was one-horse, open; the horse had bells on its back; at Eagle Nest "Jingle Bells" described the real world, and all things seemed possible.

Although I learned only a few words of Russian as a child, when I was at Eagle Nest the language seemed to engulf me. It was like growing up on an island in a river, without ever knowing how to swim. The language was linked in my mind with feastlike meals and horseback riding, with songs, airplanes, laughter. Even the Sergievskys' dog, Laska, responded only to commands in Russian: *"Idi syuda!"* (Come here!) At times it was frustrating when other people, especially children, could talk to each other in this secret tongue and I couldn't understand. But if during the rest of the year, on a New

York street or in a railway station somewhere, I heard someone speaking Russian, I listened happily, reminded of an entire hidden world which I alone knew.

Later, when as a young man I studied the language, battling its exasperating declensions and preposterous double-rooted verbs, I began to find, as I laboriously mouthed out the strange-looking words on the grammar book's page, phrases I remembered hearing used at Eagle Nest to urge on a horse, propose a toast, greet a friend. It was as if, stepping into that river at last, I did know how to swim a few strokes, after all.

X

The cardinal sin for one of Father's guests at Eagle Nest, even worse than getting visibly drunk or talking about business at the table, was to fail to write a thank-you letter. People who did not write thank-you letters were not asked back. Once when I was a teenager I had a few friends for a weekend visit; carefully briefed by me, several of them wrote afterward, but one forgot. For twenty years Father referred to that: "What is —— doing now? You know, after that weekend, I never heard from him."

When I graduated from one school I went to, Father asked me who my best teachers had been, and he wrote them thanking them for what they had done for me—a nice gesture. But when one of them failed to thank *him* for his thank-you letter, he again remembered, for decades, whenever the man's name came up: "You know, after I wrote to him that time, he never . . . "

Father always saved the thank-you letters he received from his weekend guests. All my life he would show me or send me a little bundle of them every month or two, as if to say: Here is documentary *proof* that people really are grateful to me. Thank you so much, dearest Harold, for your warm hospitality, for your gracious thoughtfulness in asking us, for the chance to meet such interesting people, for the boat ride, the cross-country skiing, the riding, the swimming; thank you, thank you, thank you, thank you . . .

No Marxist has yet written an analysis of the role of thank-you letters in ruling-class hegemony, but to whoever undertakes that task, I offer one thought: ritualistic thanking legitimates the distinction between haves and have-nots. A gift is thus a *gift,* and not a sharing of goods which were distributed unfairly in the first place. In our family, the obsession went far back: some letters that survive from the 1880s are thank-you notes written in the old, Gothic German script. But Father's brooding over unreceived thank-you letters could not be explained only in class terms: there was clearly some deeper, more painful layer as well. Throughout my childhood it remained a mystery to me.

The reverse side of Father's need to be host and giver was that he didn't like being a guest or recipient. With rare exceptions, he refused invitations to stay in someone else's home. If he was visiting another city or country to see friends or relatives, he preferred to stay in a hotel, always the fanciest available, where he could have *them* to dinner. He didn't like receiving gifts. Once my mother gave him a surprise party for his birthday. "Oh my *God,*" he said in dismay when she flung open the door to reveal twenty people singing "Happy Birthday." He made her promise never to do anything like it again. After that he usually managed to be traveling on his birthday, so there was less risk that anyone would give him anything. And although my mother chose gifts sensitively, and greatly enjoyed finding just the right one, he made her stop giving him Christmas presents.

Father liked "taking" people to dinner and the theater in New York, and grew impatient with me when I resisted going. He became uneasy anytime he could not be the giver. He was inept with anything mechanical; once when a passing driver stopped to help us change a flat tire on the highway, Father looked distraught, almost despairing, when the stranger refused his outstretched hand full of bills in payment.

Father rewarded his servants and the people who worked for him well, not so much in salary, but in trips, Christmas checks, favors for their families, extra presents that required thanking. In his younger years in The Company, he personally handed out bonus checks to employees at the year's end. Always my mother was the admiring audience, the one-person chorus of praise from the side, talking about how Father had made a "*very* generous present" to X or "was able to *do* something very handsome" for Y.

He looked for ways of introducing gifts and thanking into every possible relationship. He gave donations to friends' pet charities, usually unasked. Whenever he started seeing a new doctor, he found out if the man was associated with any research project, then sent it a big check at Christmas. World War II was the one period in his later life when he was under someone else's authority; several times he told me with great satisfaction about how, in the newly liberated Paris of 1944, he had managed to get a difficult-to-obtain restaurant reservation and take his commanding general to dinner.

He pressed gifts on people relentlessly: once he insisted on buying an expensive piece of jewelry for a friend's teenage daughter, jewelry she kept insisting she didn't want. She was embarrassed for days. There was a characteristic expression Father had when making a gift—whether slipping a folded ten-dollar bill into a headwaiter's hand or inviting a friend for an expenses-paid trip around the world—a nervous, lips-pursed, half-embarrassed smile. There was something almost erotic in his intense, urgent need for the pleasure of being thanked.

There was often an anxiously defensive tone in Father's gift-giving. If he thought he had inadvertently hurt someone's feelings, he made up for it with presents and invitations. Indeed, some of his guests were people he was afraid would be offended if they were *not* asked. "We better have the N——s on New Year's weekend, dearie," he would say to my mother. "We had them last year and the year before." For years he agonized about firing an incompetent business associate; the man was an Ivy League WASP of the kind Father most aspired to be friends with. At last he did the deed, but then redoubled his invitations to the man to visit Eagle Nest with his family. Just as Father could be easily hurt by the lack of a thank-you letter, so he seemed to feel himself in constant danger of giving offense to other people. Being the source of a flow of gifts gave him protection.

Father preferred giving gifts that were officially anonymous but in fact not so. He had great scorn, for instance, for people who gave money to universities so that lecture halls or libraries would be named after them. This was being pushy, undignified. But at the same time, when he gave money, he wanted people to find out, and he was upset if they did not.

For example, when I was old enough to go away to boarding school, Father was the major contributor to a program at the school which sent a small group of students to a Third World country each summer. I was selected to go to Africa on the first of these trips, and so out of consideration for me, Father's gift was anonymous. But he made sure everybody got the message by taking our group of students out to a lavish dinner the night before we left the country. He continued to seem frustrated that his donation had to be confidential. The fall after we returned, he attended an evening at school at which the teacher who led the group and several of us who had gone gave talks and showed slides. Afterward, enigmatically, Father told the teacher and the school's headmaster, "When you have time, there's something I'd like to talk to you about."

Eagerly—perhaps expecting more largesse—they traveled to see him some weeks later. It turned out that what Father wanted to tell them was that at any future such evenings they should say something to thank "those who had made the trip possible." Even though he, the principal donor, could not be named!

This compulsion of Father's was like a wound that never quite healed. My mother was always the intermediary, telling me privately that he was hurt when I hadn't thanked him enough for something: "I think Father's wondering, dear, if you noticed that he ordered the special chocolates he knows you like."

Once at the start of a Christmas vacation at Eagle Nest he gave me a present: a handsome poker for the fireplace in my room. I mumbled a thanks I knew was insufficient. Each day I woke and saw the poker standing there, a tangible reminder that I should say something more to him, and that he was surely waiting for this. Each day I couldn't bring myself to do so, and that made it worse—as if still more interest were accumulating on an unpaid debt. It was a great relief to go back to boarding school at the vacation's end.

There was no one with whom I could talk about these feelings. Nobody else seemed to see all that lay behind

Father's gift-giving. Most people, of course, were genuinely grateful for the presents, the unexpected checks,
the evenings at the theater or the weekends in the Adirondacks. Eagle Nest was filled with people praising Father's generosity. That made it difficult for me to be
angry with him, to feel *un*grateful, to share with anyone
my knowledge that there was an underside to all this, an
obligation to be the grateful inferior; and that the greater
was Father's gift, the more strongly was this condition
attached to it.

XI

Nowhere did Father more enjoy his role as giver than as the host of a three-day house party at Eagle Nest. We usually had a dozen or more guests each weekend. They swam and rode and ate with us, and were often transported, packed into the Chris-Craft speedboat, to cocktail parties at friends' summer houses on the next lake: "Come Saturday at six, and bring all your guests" was the leisured Adirondack style.

The guests came in many varieties. People ranked, so to speak, on a scale of guestness:

At one end of the scale were those who were employed by my parents or the Sergievskys, but who still took their meals with us at the main table in the Club House, and not with the cooks and maids in the kitchen. In this category were my governess of the moment; my cousin Kira's governess, Mrs. Gretchina; and Boris's co-pilot, Elmourza Natirboff, the stable groom's son, who helped Boris fly the plane up from New York for the weekend and then stayed with us until they flew back.

At a somewhat higher degree of guestness, which included, for example, the privilege of calling Father by his first name, was another group of people for whom he was more a client than an employer: his lawyer, his doctor, his broker. In this rank of guestness also, on certain special occasions when they were invited in for a drink with the family, were the Russians who worked at Eagle Nest: Colonel Natirboff from the stable, or the aristocratic Mrs. Phillipoff from the kitchen. They were always addressed by first name and patronymic, as they addressed Boris, Boris Vasilievich, in the respectful Russian fashion.

In another class of guests, ranking ostensibly higher but in fact lower, were certain people of high status in the outside world: a newly appointed officer of The Company, say, or someone who had made a contribution to the regional history museum Father had started, to whom he had said, "You must come and visit us sometime at our place in the Adirondacks," adding later, to my mother, "You won't like him, dearie, but don't worry. We just have to have him this once."

In the highest category of guest was an extraordinary variety of friends, most of them asked back year after year, so that there gradually grew in New York City an informal network of people who had gotten to know each other on Eagle Nest weekends. There were really two intersecting networks: Boris's friends from Manhattan's large community of exiled Russians, a few of whom he had known in the old country, and my parents' friends. It was a strange mix of cultures. After dinner Boris's friends sometimes remained at the table, ending an evening swaying back and forth with arms linked, in a Russian song. My parents' friends were more likely to end up discussing over coffee whether Eisenhower was pursuing the right policy on the Berlin Question.

Of the Russians there were the Kalbouss family—he played the accordion at a Russian restaurant in New York; Colonel Zouboff, who gave Russian lessons at Berlitz; Prince and Princess Bagration—he was a direct descendant of the General Bagration who appears in *War and Peace*; and Nicholas de Transehe, who had been, I was told, an Arctic explorer in old Russia. He thrilled me deeply by taking a scientific interest in the model airplanes I built. Orest Sergievsky, Boris's grown son by his first marriage in Russia, visited us on occasional weekends: he was a warm, ebullient man with a wide circle of friends—artists, musicians, singers, dancers. The ballerina Maria Tallchief was not Russian, but came often because she was married to Boris's co-pilot, Elmourza Natirboff; she sometimes did a few dance steps for us after dinner. Among the Russians it was their rank in the old world that counted, not their station in the new. One visitor to Eagle Nest, a princess who was related to the Imperial Family, signed our guest book simply as "Vera of Russia."

Finally, at the dim horizon of my memory, was the one time I touched the hand that had touched the hand of God: a visit from Alexandra Tolstoy. The great man's youngest daughter, she had been his secretary at the end of his life. She was among the few of his numerous legitimate and illegitimate children to side with him in the wild quarrels he had with his wife. At the age of eighty-two Tolstoy ran away from home and fell ill on the journey; as he died in the humble stationmaster's house at Astapovo while the whole world watched, Alexandra was at his side. If there is any guest at Eagle Nest whom I would want to resurrect from the dead and talk to, it would be she. Alexandra Tolstoy was there only when I was very small. She went into the woods and gathered wild mushrooms for the table, mushrooms which no one at Eagle Nest since then has ever been able to identify or find.

. . .

From my parents' friends, entries in our guest book overflowed with verses celebrating flaming hearths and autumn colors, plum puddings and rides in the woods. There were names in Chinese characters, hyphenated names from England, snapshots pasted in of guests skiing or swimming or posing in a group on the wide stone front steps of the Club House, comments from a thousand weekends:

Jotsiens in Suid Afrika . . .

−40 degrees outside; 100 proof inside.

> *La neige a tout couvert, et je prie*
> *Dans cet océan blanc, où la vie*
> *Se recueille; et bientôt l'horizon*
> *Se couvrira de fleurs . . . Chère maison amie*
> *Qui nous protège tous de la froide saison!*

The latter lines were from a long, flowery ode, which went on for many stanzas, by Père Junod, a cheerful, energetic, Swiss-born pastor who was, bizarrely, the chief chaplain of the South African prison system. One of his jobs was to accompany men to the scaffold when they were hanged, something which then, as now, took place in South Africa with great frequency. As was the case with many of my parents' guests (some of whom came to our house in Princeton, though most to Eagle Nest), Father had met and taken a liking to him while traveling.

There were many others from Africa: prime ministers black and white, American diplomats, dissident journalists, Quakers, a young man who was tutor to the grandchildren of the Emperor of Ethiopia, and David Stirling, a British war hero who now waged a lonelier battle for racial justice in Rhodesia. From England came various distant relatives of my mother's, an odd assortment of brigadiers and gentleman farmers, who signed the guest book with addresses like Ravenscroft or Brentwood Manor. Three awed Soviet seismologists came for lunch one day when they were visiting the Adirondacks to study earthquakes.

Of the American guests, there were some whose names chartmakers of this country's upper social reaches would recognize, but many more they wouldn't: pleasant people with gracious voices redolent of wide, shady streets in the suburbs of Boston or of old stone farmhouses in Connecticut. They were often childhood friends of my mother's, who asked: "And where are you now, Adam?" as if my progress through boarding school, college, military service, work, marriage, was all a predictable trajectory, and they needed only to fix exactly how many degrees I was from start or finish.

Then, because the most admirable of Father's eccentricities was his open-minded sense of politics, there were people like Adlai Stevenson, George Kennan, and the socialist leader Norman Thomas. Father would ask their opinions on various questions of the day, listening respectfully in that familiar position of his, hand supporting chin, first and second fingers over his mouth.

Charles Y. came for many weekends, a man who everybody knew was CIA, but in those days you weren't supposed to talk about it. Barney S. was another frequent visitor, who, I came to realize some years later, was The Company's liaison man with "The Agency." Michael N. was an executive whose attractive young wife was discovered in Boris's arms in the boathouse. Sidney L. was a pompous college president who was so haughty with the kitchenmaids that they slipped Ex-Lax into his coffee.

Barry A. and Susan F. were in their twenties. For years he courted her; she couldn't decide. Ever a hopeful matchmaker, my mother rooted for them to marry, asking them together on weekends, hoping that if they just had a good enough time with each other it would solve everything. He took her for moonlight canoe rides; from my bed at night I could hear the splash of paddles and the indistinct murmur of their voices over the lake. I imagined him pleading, her wavering. It seemed that their courtship, like my childhood, was suspended in time, and that it would go on forever, and each summer they would be there for an Eagle Nest weekend and go canoeing while my mother said, "Poor girl, I wish she would make up her mind." But one day he gave up, and married someone else.

Father remained loyal to his relatives. And to a group of people he seemed to place in the same category: half a dozen German-Jewish friends from his childhood, and their children and grandchildren. But except for these people—and for the stray Jew who unavoidably turned up as someone's date or spouse—there were almost no Jews among the guests at Eagle Nest. In Father's cosmopolitan taste in friendships, this was the only significant exception.

There were certain rituals to an Eagle Nest weekend. This was a time for relaxed talk, never for the making of deals. And, in three slow-paced days, the guests could get to know each other fairly well: that was the greatest luxury of all. That part of the dinner table conversation in Russian was beyond Father's control, but for what went on in English, he set the tone: serious but not argumentative, entertaining but not bawdy—if someone told an off-color joke, his polite laugh had an ice edge to it. He was a good host, though, sitting at the head of the table in riding boots and a worn suede jacket, discreetly dropping enough information about each guest's background to encourage others to ask more. From his end of the table he presided over the arrangements for horseback riding, invited people for motorboat excursions, and handed out free passes to the museum.

Sometimes the wealthy collect art or sculpture; my parents did, but only as an afterthought. Mostly they collected people. They did it well. There are worse hobbies. Even though I came to be dismayed by the style in which they lived, their friends were the best part. Sooner or later anyone they wanted to get to know better was invited to Eagle Nest. If he or she was asked back the following summer, it was a stamp of approval. On this little island of good fellowship the African journalists mixed with the Russian countesses with surprising ease; for a brief moment it was enough to make one think that all people could do the same everywhere.

XII

If I had to date the end of my childhood from one moment, it would be when, at age thirteen, I decided to go away to boarding school. Knowing that I was far too tightly bound to my now-aging mother, always fearing Father's disapproval, and feeling socially crippled by my various phobias, I groped toward the only avenue in our protected existence which seemed to lead to a more independent life.

Surprisingly, it did so. In the four years on a Connecticut hilltop that followed, I came alive. I entered the school as a boy who read books; I left as one who, in some rudimentary way, thought about them. I learned that words meant more than their surfaces, and that music could say things words could not. For the first time in my life I formed a few friendships that had not been arranged by my mother, nurtured with invitations to Eagle Nest. And I learned, though exposed to only a narrow and unrepresentative slice of the world, that it was made up of classes who often hated and envied each other.

The conflict in a New England prep school is not between bourgeoisie and proletariat, but it is a class conflict nonetheless. The students were all white, all male, and mostly wealthy: a year's tuition bill was higher than a junior faculty salary. From that discrepancy came a subdued tension. My teachers had generally gone to public schools themselves; most had worked their way through college or gone on the G.I. bill. They often took summer jobs to make ends meet, while the students they taught vacationed in Paris or in the Hamptons. In the dining hall the teachers' faces wore silent, watchful expressions as they listened to students talk about visiting the Riviera or buying new sports cars.

One day a teacher told me that he had found a boy throwing away a brand-new pair of pants, right out of the package, into a dormitory trash barrel.

"Why?" the horrified teacher asked.

"Oh," the boy said, "I ordered this suit because I wanted the coat. I don't need the pants."

This little episode reverberated, I think, because it was the first time I saw my own class through the eyes of another. It was as if I gradually acquired a new lens with which to see the concentric circles of privilege in which I lived. I read the alumni newsletter and saw the array of big law firms and corporations almost all graduates seemed to end up in. I noticed that the school's board of trustees held most of its meetings not on campus but at a bank in New York.

Most instructive of all was that while I was there the school was, beneath its ivied walls and stained-glass chapel windows, the scene of a political battle. I began to see that the adult world did not have a united front. The typical trustee of Pomfret School was a Hartford insurance executive or Philadelphia banker, whose definition of a good school was one that most closely resembled the dear old Pomfret he had attended forty years before. But our headmaster was in many ways an admirable and progressive man, especially for a complacent decade like the fifties. He wanted to make the school coed, to admit blacks, and to put less emphasis on athletics. To most of the trustees in their bank boardroom these hopes seemed positively Bolshevik. The crowning outrage came when he tried to hire a non-Episcopalian as chaplain. The long-simmering conflict exploded and the headmaster resigned. These battles seem antiquated now, but the issues were symbolic, and at the time they loomed very large for me.

I also began to notice how my classmates conceived of the borders of life's possibilities, and how they seemed to assume the world belonged to them. In a way it did. A few years after I graduated, two members of a class just older than mine wrote to the alumni newsletter about how they had met again—in Vietnam. One was in the State Department, the other with a large construction firm building military bases. Over cool drinks on a Saigon patio, they said, they had talked about all that had happened "since the Class of '58 was loosed upon the world."

Around the same time I ran into a fellow alumnus and asked him what he had been doing:

"Well," he said cheerfully, "after college and the army I went into investment banking. First Boston. But now"—he threw his hands wide in a gesture of benign, tolerant acceptance of his own rashness—"I've gone *clear* to the other end of the spectrum. I'm a stockbroker."

My life up to this point is documented with hundreds, no, thousands, of photographs taken by my mother, stuffed into drawers, overflowing from boxes and closet shelves at Eagle Nest. From prep school on, though, there are few, for I was away from home. But if I could snap a few scenes for an imaginary album, here is what they might be:

My last year at boarding school. I have been a diligent student, good at languages, encouraged by teachers to give little speeches in the daily assembly on the crisis in the Middle East or whatever. One day the headmaster, a man of great enthusiasm, is talking to me. "For every boy here," he says, "I like to imagine that we're helping him go in a particular direction, a direction *he* is best suited for. For you, I've thought it might be the State Department, or something in that realm." Suddenly, in a thunderclap of revelation, I know that whatever I do with my life, it will *not* be in that "realm." So: despite everything teachers and parents say about how I'm free to choose, they have a plan for me after all. I cannot yet see that plan clearly, but I suddenly become wary.

A visit home on a school vacation. When my parents enter the front door, I am astonished that Rex comes in with them. Ever since we had gotten him, my parents had made him stay in a doghouse outdoors. If he came in, they had said, he would shed fur on the rug, steal food, tip over vases, spread fleas. But now, in my absence, he has conquered them. Father, particularly, has grown sentimental about Rex, who now sleeps on a mat in his study. In a few more years, Father will get him a small cot, saying that there are drafts on the floor. He spends long minutes stroking Rex's yellow fur and talking to him.

A summer job during college. At Father's insistence, I am working three months in a Wall Street brokerage house. "Even if you're not going to do this kind of thing for a career, you ought to know how it works." A reasonable thought, perhaps, but figures about price-earnings ratios and discount commissions evaporate as soon as I take them in. I befriend the "messenger boy" in the section where I'm a clerk: he is a black man, eighty-five years old. Gum-chewing office workers in their thirties call him "John" and tell him to take papers here and there. I ask him his life story; it turns out that as a teen-ager in the Navy he went round the world on Theodore Roosevelt's Great White Fleet. He is pleased I've read about this. I call him "Professor" and avoid asking him to run messages. At the end of the summer, he says: "Thank you for calling me 'Professor.' "

Once, during these years, Father arranged for the two of us to make a long trip to the Soviet Union. It was as if he wanted to claim Russia for himself, and not cede it all to Boris. Perennially fascinated with languages, he had decided that we would use the trip to study Russian. Maybe unconsciously he hoped that working together on one of the most foreign of foreign tongues, we might at last be able to speak to each other.

As we flew off to Moscow, I felt the old irrational terror: I would be isolated in strange places with him; what if I had nausea attacks and was not able to eat for weeks at a time? But this anxiety was soon replaced by others. To teach us Russian (which we had already been studying for a month or so beforehand), Father had asked for two guides to travel with us, one to give private lessons to each of us. Intourist, the Soviet agency that deals with foreign travelers, could not understand why a pair of tourists needed two guides, and provided only one. Father made vigorous protests to various officials and fired off telegrams, and finally a second guide was dispatched from headquarters.

The two of them were with us for two months. They gave us lessons each morning and evening, and Father insisted that we speak Russian with them at lunch and dinner as well. These meals were particularly horrendous: Soviet restaurants were slow; the guides were afraid to talk about anything controversial; our own limited Russian vocabularies petered out before we were through the soup. What made everything especially absurd was that the two guides spoke almost faultless English, which they were frustrated at not being able to practice.

Intourist procedure dictated that tourists traveling at the deluxe rate have, in each city outside Moscow, a local guide as well as anyone accompanying them from the capital. And so in a string of half a dozen cities across that vast country, puzzled officials in hotels from Tashkent to Tbilisi huddled and whispered at the sight of two tourists with three guides, all of this confirming, no doubt, what Soviet schoolchildren are told about the extravagance of American capitalists. Furthermore, the two guides traveling with us meant more luggage (Father always traveled with half a dozen pieces to begin with). Thus our entourage of guides and baggage, theirs and ours, was so big that two limousines had to meet us at each airport.

Though fascinated by the country, I felt sunk in a morass of embarrassment at our lavish style of traveling. Though annoyed by Soviet prohibitions against tipping, Father enjoyed the trip. We met few Russians, however. In addition to the formidable barrier of guides and limousines, Father's uphill struggle to learn the language did not, curiously, include much of a desire to speak it with anyone other than our teachers—either in the USSR or at Eagle Nest, which had of course been full of Russian speakers for years. For him a language was not a pathway but an acquisition; in this respect he was like someone who collects books mainly to collect them, not to read them.

When the trip was over and we parted ways in an airport, I saw on his face the reverse side of my nausea: his expectation, his hope, his implicit demand that I thank him and give him the kiss on the cheek that symbolized my gratitude. I did so, but felt trapped, said something ambiguous that I knew fell short of what he wanted, and turned away.

A visit home from college. For several years now, since graduating from prep school and entering Harvard, I have rarely brought friends to Eagle Nest. I am afraid of their being overwhelmed by it; I want new friends to know me as *me,* and not as someone indelibly connected to a piece of property. Father is hurt by this. At last, in response to his repeated urgings—"Why don't we ever get to meet your friends?"—I bring four college classmates for the weekend.

They are polite to my parents, but Father is distant and reserved. I get that old, guilty, before-the-thunderstorm feeling, but don't know what the trouble is. *Something* is clearly terribly wrong, and I'm at fault. In the weeks that follow, I open each letter from him with a feeling of dread, but still there is no clue.

Two months later, on my next visit home, my parents and I are at the dining table. Father says, "Adam, could you come to my study after lunch? There's something I've been wanting to talk to you about."

That clammy fear again. I lose my appetite. To keep

the conversation going, my mother brightly talks about other things. After the meal he and I go up to his study.

Once again he is at his desk, which is laden with the symbols of his power in the world—briefcase, Dictaphone, copper paperweights. He pauses for a moment before beginning, looking into space, composing his thoughts into the exact phrasing he wants. Then he swivels his chair to face me. I am twenty but feel six.

"Adam, I've been concerned, very concerned about something these last few months."

" . . . Yes?"

"I've been worried about the friendships you've been making at college. You know, Harvard's a very cosmopolitan place, but I don't think you've been taking advantage of it."

"What do you mean? I don't understand."

"Well, those four boys you brought home a few months ago. They were all Jewish. Every one of them."

"But what . . . ? That never occurred to me. . . . I don't pick my friends that way."

"I'm just wondering if you aren't unconsciously prejudiced against *non*-Jews in some way."

"*What?* That's ridiculous!"

We argue fruitlessly. Father is obsessed by this piece of evidence, and refers to it repeatedly over the next year or two. I am baffled. The argument continues by mail after I return to college. I mentally inventory my friends ethnically, something I had not done before. Plenty are not Jewish. Why is he so upset? A few months later my parents visit Cambridge and I invite some friends to my room to meet them, making sure Father spends most of his time talking to one who is indisputably Anglo-Saxon. The same is true of several girls I later bring home for weekends. I defend myself articulately, in letters and talk, pointing to this friend and that as indications that I've been unjustly accused, and don't have any problem about non-Jews. It does not yet occur to me that he's the one with the problem.

XIII

In the summer after my first year at college, I went along with Father on one of his business trips to Africa. We stayed in guest villas in Company mining towns, but also visited a number of offices of a new organization Father had helped start: the African-American Institute. The Institute had somehow acquired a great deal of money; it was a foundation that brought large numbers of African students to the United States and sent American teachers to Africa. Its ultimate purpose was to ensure that the elite of newly independent English-speaking Africa would be trained in America, and thus more open to doing business with the United States. Father was chairman of the board, as he usually was of anything he became involved with. Everywhere we went, the Institute's field represen tatives, eager to please, met us at the airport.

Father traveled with memos prepared by officials of the Institute or The Company, giving little capsule biographies of people we were scheduled to meet at dinner parties: "Mr. Marube is in his late thirties. Educated in England. Protégé of Minister of Commerce. May run for Parliament from Nizamba district. Friendly, intelligent, and ambitious."

At the end of our travels together he headed home, and I continued southward, to South Africa. I had begun to read about the country; my imagination had been caught by the stark injustice of apartheid, and by the drama and heroism of the resistance to it: the great marches and demonstrations, the bus boycotts where thousands of black people walked many miles to work rather than pay an increased fare. It was a society where the sides seemed clear: right and wrong were absolutely unmistakable, and that appealed to me greatly.

Something else drew me to South Africa as well, although I could not see it clearly at the time. The Company's main African holdings were elsewhere, but some were in South Africa itself. South Africa was the continent's industrial heart, and Father's trips always began or ended in Johannesburg. With its vast extremes of wealth and poverty compressed into one country, I think South Africa had come to represent for me in purest form the pattern of worldwide inequity from which I had benefited so much.

Before long I reached the continent's end, Cape Town. And there, because a friend had given me his phone number, I chanced to meet a man who was to have a considerable effect on my life. Patrick Duncan, although white, was in the front lines of South Africa's movement for racial equality. He was the editor of a biweekly antiapartheid newspaper, was angrily denounced by the government, and was one of the handful of white people invited to speak to mass black protest rallies. In the past ten years he had been jailed three times for his beliefs. Yet paradoxically—and this was partly what made me feel a sudden bond with him—Duncan had come to all this from the top of his country's elite: his father had been a Cabinet minister and Governor General. His life seemed proof that you could do battle for justice even if you had been born on the wrong side.

I spent a day with him at the newspaper he ran. Two

security policemen sat on a park bench near the building's door, dourly eyeing everyone who came in. I sat in on a staff meeting, over a lunch of sandwiches, pickles, and beer, and heard the paper's black street salesmen talk about how they were harassed by police. A ruddy-faced man with an impeccable Oxford accent, Patrick Duncan ran the meeting, speaking emphatically, precisely, always in complete sentences. He wore a coat and tie at all times. He spoke with great intensity, as if constantly thinking: there is little time, little time; we must get right to the point.

I sensed that I had something to learn from Duncan, but it was not until years later that I really understood what it was: unlike me, he was not weighed down by a sense of guilt, or by the effort of trying to deny his origins. He was driven only by a burning passion for justice.

On this particular day, the staff meeting went on to discuss an American naval flotilla then making a "goodwill visit" to Cape Town. To everyone's dismay, the U.S. Navy was putting its sailors ashore in racially segregated groups, so as not to offend their white South African hosts. "If only," Duncan said in that earnest way of his, "if only I could get out there and *talk* to the admiral. I'm sure I could make him understand."

That evening he and I stayed up late talking politics, walking on the lawn of his house to get away from any eavesdropping microphones which might be indoors. The night was warm; the dim bulk of Table Mountain loomed in the background. *"Your country,"* Duncan said, as he paced back and forth, "your country holds *this* country in the palm of its hand."

He turned and looked at me. "You're an American. You've been to South Africa now and seen apartheid firsthand. You've got an important message to tell people when you get home."

For a young college student, this was heady stuff. That night I sat for a long time on a seawall near where I was staying in Cape Town, watching the ocean waves pound, unable to sleep.

At the end of a second evening at his house, Duncan asked if on my next summer vacation from college I would come back to South Africa and work for his paper, and of course I said yes.

My parents strongly resisted the plan. Father grew heated: "Adam, I really think this is a *bad* idea. It could be dangerous. And there's not much an outsider can do to solve South Africa's problems."

"If you won't pay my fare to South Africa," I said, "I'll take a part-time job during school and earn the money myself."

This odd threat worked, and they relented.

When I arrived back in South Africa the next summer, the country was in turmoil. The underground African National Congress had turned to sabotage for the first time, setting off bombs in various cities, and the white government rushed through draconian new laws in response. After a nationwide manhunt, banner headlines proclaimed the arrest of Nelson Mandela. There were rumors of general strikes and uprisings to come.

I was filled with dreams of becoming a crusading reporter in a country with scandals waiting to be exposed on all sides. But things turned out otherwise. Patrick Duncan, expecting imminent house arrest, had been forced to flee the country and was writing his newspaper editorials from just across the border. The staff remain-

ing in Cape Town thought I would be deported immediately if I was too visible as a reporter or was seen at the
paper's office, so I worked in my tiny, cramped rented
room. I mainly copyedited articles and corrected the English of Africans who wrote letters to the editor. The letters made up in feeling what they lacked in grammar, and
I left the basic wording pretty much alone:

> Sir:
> Although I am small, I am pulling a heavy wagon.
> Whenever we give for freedom we must forget our
> differences. . . . If we are too critical amongst our-
> selves it gives the enemy a chance to be strong. . . .
> Anyone who breaks through the iron chains of
> oppression must be heartily welcomed by all Parties,
> as long as his manifesto is "Africa must be free!"

Or:

> Sir:
> Although our being tongue-tied by our oppressors
> and colonial powers hinders our progress towards
> freedom . . . I feel that justice will eat up injustice
> until one day injustice falls dramatically dead.

Images from the summer:
Headlines in the white papers: CHAIRMAN OF RUGBY
BOARD LODGES COMPLAINT ON QUALITY OF SPORTS COM-
MENTATORS; 400,000 WHITES FLEE ALGERIA; S.A. BEAUTY
QUEEN SAYS ENGLAND "NICE BUT COLD." The Johannesburg railroad station—a vast, modernistic structure with
a graceful vaulting roof, but all built, at great expense, so
that white and black passengers never meet. The slogans
on walls everywhere: AVENGE SHARPEVILLE! FREE MAN-

DELA! Six months in jail if you're caught slogan-writing. A morning scene in Johannesburg: a garden wall painted on the night before; a white matron in a white dress, hands on hips, supervising a black servant whitewashing over the offending words.

In the *Cape Times,* an article on the "banning" of 102 people under new legislation running side by side with a story on Yves St. Laurent's new collection. A parade through the streets of Johannesburg of white mercenary "freedom fighters," who had been battling the leftist government of the Congo. Little everyday things one would take for granted elsewhere that here, on the verge of race war, seem suddenly absurd: the orchestra conductor's formal black tailcoat at a concert, a newsstand displaying the *Journal of the South African Racing Pigeon Society.*

At one point I have to take a trip through an impoverished, overcrowded rural area. I hitchhike; then, when the road gives out, I go two days by horseback, past eroded scars of red earth and the broad blackened paths of grass fires. On the dusty mountain path I pass dozens of somber-faced black men without work, walking many miles to the recruiting offices for the mines: ahead of them lies an examination by company doctors—is this piece of human machinery fit for backbreaking work? If so, then ten or eleven months away from your family; a bunk in a crowded barracks; work shifts in a hot, dangerous cacophony of drills and conveyor belts a mile under the earth.

Sometimes a passing man who speaks English hails me with the ritual greeting of these mountains, long and drawn out: "Where . . . are . . . you . . . coming . . . from?" I answer with the name of the town I have just left. I do not give the larger answer, as I do not to almost everyone I meet this summer. For it is not impossible that one of these men, wearing a blanket around his shoulders and a conical straw hat against the sun, frowning curiously at this white stranger on the rocky trail, will end up working in a Company mine.

Where are you coming from? In more subtle dimensions, the question kept recurring. Looking today over a predictably indignant newspaper article I wrote after I returned to the United States, I see that I left out every experience that raised it. Here is one:

I am crossing South Africa from west to east. I have reached a town in one of the desolate "Bantustan" areas set aside for blacks. The following day I have an appointment to do an interview in the city of Durban. I have a twenty-four-hour journey ahead of me: all day on a bus, which connects to an overnight train to Durban. I show up at the bus depot early in the morning. But as the bus rolls in, I realize that I missed something in the timetable. For on the side of the bus is a sign:

SLEGS VIR NEI BLANKES
NON-EUROPEANS ONLY.

Almost all South African transport is segregated, and in this part of the country there are many more black buses than white. The only white bus on this route, it turns out, comes too late to connect with my train.

I explain my predicament to an unsmiling Afrikaner official at the bus depot. He shakes his head. The law is the law. "Ag, man, you just must wait."

Meanwhile, the white driver of the blacks-only bus I had hoped to take overhears my pleading. He confers with his ticket taker, also white. Then he turns to me and says, "All right, mate. Come along with us. We're breaking the rules by taking you. We could get in trouble. So don't tell anyone."

The two of them sit in a little compartment at the front of the bus, walled off like an airliner's cockpit. The ticket collector insists on giving up his seat for me, and sits on an upturned crate. At stops, he opens the door into the rest of the bus, collects ticket money, then shuts the door and sits down again. Both men are Afrikaners. They insist on giving me food and cigarettes. They could not be more generous, and I am touched and grateful for the ride. They ask my impressions of South Africa. I try to stay off politics, and talk about how spectacular the scenery is. And it is: gentle hills rolling away from us on both sides toward a horizon that in Africa always seems wider and more distant than any other horizon in the world.

Suddenly, in midafternoon, some sort of scuffle breaks out among the African passengers. An argument, shouting. The ticket collector, a strong, husky man, lets out an oath in Afrikaans, gets up, and goes through the door into the passenger compartment. He picks up one of the two arguing black passengers by the back of his shirt collar, spins him around, and gives him a brutally hard kick in the buttocks that sends the man sprawling to the far end of the aisle. Then he turns around, comes back to our little cabin in front, and shuts the door.

The bus doesn't stop. The ticket collector and driver resume talking: rugby, weather, movie actresses. I feel a strange terror, not at having been the object of violence but at having *not* been. I feel I should do something, say something, get off the bus. But we are on a remote country highway, many miles from the nearest town. Our conversation continues, awkwardly, until they leave me off at the railroad station in time to catch my train. I thank them profusely, remembering once again that they had risked getting into trouble for my sake because I was a fellow white man.

One of Patrick Duncan's quirks, for which he was often criticized by fellow activists, was that he was wildly, exuberantly pro-American. He was convinced that President Kennedy could be persuaded to put strong pressure on South Africa to change its ways. At first I shared this idea: if you could only get the ear of the right people and explain things, I thought, surely the United States would at last live up to its heritage and come out in support of the antiapartheid movement. It was an attractive scenario, above all because it offered me a role. I prepared lists of people to talk to when I got home—influential journalists, people Father knew in the government, foundation executives.

But gradually I saw how hopeless this project was. Why expect the United States to square off against a country where it has huge investments? And which is so staunchly anti-Communist?

It is hard to fix a moment when my understanding of all this began—which meant seeing that most international politics works in economic and not moral terms. Although I do remember standing at the directory board in the lobby of the American Embassy in Pretoria, and being astonished by the long list of military attachés we had there. One result of that summer was that I do not think in terms of that "we" anymore, identifying myself with the U.S. government. As in "Why are we in Vietnam?'' When *that* question came up a few years later, I didn't believe the White House answers. South Africa helped me lose my political virginity.

It sounds as if I got far from home that summer. This was both true and not true. For this whole trip was the first major step I had taken in my life totally against Father's will, and that had required great emotional effort. In midsummer, on one of his regular business trips to Africa, Father came to see me for a few hours to make sure I was all right, and to say that he still thought the whole venture was a bad idea. In a restaurant in Cape Town, I got a severe attack of the old psychosomatic nausea, as if that problem, too, had followed me to the ends of the earth.

Yet, at the same time, I learned a great deal. In South Africa it is as if you see every scene with a special kind of filter over it, which, as in infrared photography, shows you an image in terms of heat or radiation instead of the colors seen by the normal eye. The filter South Africa holds in front of the human landscape is one through which the stark contrasts of race throw into relief all the differences between wealth and poverty which in other countries may be more hidden.

I remember a short encounter with one South African that summer. It was an innocuous conversation, as we sat on bed and chair in the Johannesburg YMCA room where I was staying, but it has echoed down through the years. He was a white student, about my age. Earnest and likable, he was something of a liberal on the race issue. Had I been born in this society, I thought, I might be he. He was well-read, English-speaking; I felt immediately at ease with him.

"What," I asked him, "are you going to do with your life?" It was a question I was trying to figure out for myself.

"I've thought about it a lot," he said. "I think I'm going into the executive-trainee program at Anglo-American [the country's largest mining corporation]. There are good prospects there for someone who wants to have a solid career and raise a family."

A few minutes later, speaking of a mining executive he knew, he mentioned that the man had a fine vacation home on the beach at "Plett"—the resort town of Plettenberg Bay, on the Indian Ocean. The young student spoke in that pleasant, upbeat tone I had heard a hundred times, as my parents and their friends compared summer plans: And when are you going up to the mountains? To the Cape? To the Vineyard? July? Oh yes, it's *so* lovely then.

A flood of feeling came over me. Good prospects! A few miles away from us I've seen thousands of people living in shantytown huts made of tin and tar paper and old automobile doors. Children are big-bellied with malnutrition. How can he talk of vacation houses? But wait! Was I not heading home to one myself in a few weeks' time? I felt jarred. The moment reverberated for a long time. It felt like a fork in the road. From that point on, it seemed to me, my own path could never lead to taking Father's place, at the head of the Club House table, at Eagle Nest.

The few months I spent in South Africa were a watershed in my life. It was my first experience with people engaged in serious politics, whose beliefs were not merely opinions voiced in the classroom or at the dinner table but commitments that could affect someone's comfort, freedom, even life. One man I knew fairly well was later hanged. Another, a burly, vibrant black activist with a humorous glint in his eyes and a fine singing voice, was eventually driven out of his mind by police torture. Others were to spend years in jail. Dimly, unable to assimilate it all at the time, I had the sense that summer that I was traveling across a battlefield-to-be, talking to people who would someday be fighting on both sides of a civil war. I kept a journal, which was my first attempt to write about things that mattered. Instead of letters, I sent home a carbon copy. When I got back to Eagle Nest at the end of the summer, Father handed it back to me. He had corrected it in blue pencil, as if it were an English paper, marking errors of grammar and style.

XIV

By the time I was in college I was usually working in the summers, so my visits to Eagle Nest were for only a week or two a year. In many ways, the place was no longer the same.

As Gertrude became older, barriers seemed to grow around her—or maybe they had always been there, crashed through momentarily only by Boris, and as a small child I had not seen them. She grew fearful about living in New York, even in her elegant apartment on Central Park West, and moved her family to a supposedly safer neighborhood on the Upper East Side. She worried about robberies and rapes and muggings and other nameless dangers, and kept her phone number unlisted. Her conversation was limited to pleasantries. At the Eagle Nest table, she steered away from any topic that might lead to the slightest disagreement. She told me, "I make it a rule never to discuss politics or religion."

Sometimes this led to awkward circumlocutions. One lunchtime she told a long, complicated story that had to do with some mishap Boris had had when making a Russian-language radio broadcast in New York at election time. But she told the whole story without saying which candidate he was going on the air to endorse, because that would have raised the specter of "politics." (It was

Nelson Rockefeller, I found out later: he was tough on Communism and had once chartered Boris's plane.)

Always, earlier, I had had the sense that in the eyes of this slight, reserved woman, moving now with a slower step, there shone a deep intelligence, a dignity, an ability to understand me, a willingness to offer me support. But I was no longer a child now. If I crossed an invisible line and talked of anything that seemed too intimate—my summer in Africa, Father, Boris, her life, my plans for mine—Gertrude backed off. Wrapped in a shawl, she surrounded herself always with a protective screen of family and servants and guests, and it was impossible to speak to her alone.

The Hochschilds were a family where voices were never raised, a family where the impact of a raised eyebrow lingered for hours. And of that whole family, Gertrude was the most restrained of all. It was as if she had made one incredibly bold move, marrying Boris, and then retreated forever.

Unknown to us all, over the years something had been simmering inside her. Perhaps, understandably, it was the humiliation of Boris's unending string of love affairs. Or maybe it was that she, like me, had felt the weight of Father's disapproval—in her case, for bringing Boris into the family. Or perhaps she was envious of my parents for having, unexpectedly with their late marriage, stolen some happiness from life that had been denied to her. I still do not know.

One day in New York, she called Father and said she wanted to see him. When she arrived she was shaking with rage. No one had ever seen her like that before. No one was ever to see her like that again. She blew up and in paranoid fashion accused him: "You're stealing our friends!"

"But Gertrude," Father said, "what do you mean?" This all made little sense to him, as the two families and their guests had shared the same summer dinner table for nearly twenty years.

"People like the ——s and the ——s, whom I used to ask as my guests, now you're asking as *your* guests!"

"But Gertrude, my goodness, if I'd known—"

"I won't have it. I just won't have it! We're moving out!"

My parents were very upset, but could not persuade Gertrude to change her mind. Genial Boris seemed bewildered by his quiet wife's new rage.

For one last, uneasy summer the two families and their guests all ate at the Club House. The atmosphere was strained. No one ever mentioned a word about the blowup. Over the summer Gertrude had another house on the estate remodeled. At the table my parents would politely ask how the work was coming along. Then Gertrude moved herself, Boris, Kira, and all the visiting Russian friends to the new house, and one magical era of my childhood came to an end.

On my visits to Eagle Nest now, as I entered my twenties, I always made a ritual call on Gertrude and Boris in their new house (which included the subritual of visiting the old Russian servants in the kitchen) for my favorite meal, *pelmeni.* I was not included as a target of the strange new anger Gertrude felt toward my parents, whom she now seldom saw.

"It's too bad," she said to me about her move out of the Club House. "I felt we were just getting to know each other."

I don't think that was so, but I would have liked it to be.

Only family and a few close friends were exempt from Gertrude's formality: she continued to call everyone "Mr." and "Mrs.," including Boris's new co-pilot, who remained "Mr. Mikhailov" for the entire decade he was part of their summer household. After a while the "Mr." or "Mrs." in cases like that was so unnatural you winced a little to hear it, as if it was a sign of covert hostility. Some mysterious tension arose between Gertrude and her daughter's governess, Mrs. Gretchina, and for several years they barely spoke.

Gertrude seemed to become increasingly peevish toward Boris, as if unleashing some of the anger she must have felt at him over the years. She must have hoped that his succession of mistresses would one day cease, and that she would have him to herself at last. But this was not to be: until he died, Boris maintained a second apartment in New York, referred to as his "office."

Boris seemed resigned to Gertrude's resentment, called her "Mommy" in an affected way, and, basically, tuned out. The great weekend house parties, when a dozen of his Russian friends came to Eagle Nest, gradually ceased. Boris sang no more opera arias. It was as if the Germanic and Russian spirits had battled for control of their household, and the Germans had won.

Boris flew until he was seventy-seven; then, despite invitations for Eagle Nest vacations to the man who did the physical examinations for the Federal Aviation Administration, the doctors made him stop. He sold his beloved Grumman Mallard. From all the flying, he had grown deaf. Or *said* he had grown deaf, for he seemed to hear well if someone spoke to him in Russian, or called to him using the Russian accenting of his name, "BahREES!" With no battles to fight or planes to fly, Boris sat in their living room napping, like a caged lion, although he came to life instantly, eyes wide, head thrown back, nostrils flaring, if an attractive young woman entered the room.

Colonel Natirboff from the stable retired to Florida, but Boris kept on riding. For years Boris had come up to Eagle Nest with his co-pilot every spring to spend several days in the woods, clearing the riding trails of the trees that had fallen across them during the winter. It was as if to say: Even though I married money, I can still do rough physical work. Now, nearing eighty and with no co-pilot to help him, he cleared small logs off the trails even when he was so stiff and weak he could barely get back on his horse. Almost out of sight behind the trees, the new stable attendant followed him on the trail to make sure he was all right. After every windstorm, Boris took an ax and saw when he went out riding.

XV

If the story of Father and me were a play, it would call, at about this point in the action, for a scene of dramatic conflict. A violent argument some night in the Cottage at Eagle Nest, while a thunderstorm rages outside. Some episode—Father's marking up of my South Africa diary, say—sparks a confrontation. The shell of our decorum is broken. The two of us face each other angrily, and at last there is a climax to this painful buildup of tension.

I pound my fist on his desk and say: "Lay off! Stop telling me how to run my life! Why do you criticize everything I do? It's not just the diary, it's everything! Why?"

He grows red in the face. "Adam, you're giving it all up! Everything I've given you! You could be one of the people who *run* this country, and you're giving it all up. Yes! I *do* criticize what you do. Because you're making mistakes, mistakes, mistakes!"

To which I draw a deep breath and say: "Father, it's *you* I'm rejecting! I don't want to be like *you*!"

And so at last we are having the talk we never have had, about us. Our voices are raised higher and higher. Ever harsher words are spoken. Things are said which can never be unsaid. I storm out of the house, my angry departing footsteps crashing down the front steps. My car roars down the driveway into the storm. Father slams the door behind me. Helpless on the sidelines, my mother weeps.

But all this never happened. To slam doors, to rant and shout, was not in Father's character. Nor, for better or for worse—perhaps mostly for worse—was it in mine. We fought not like wrestlers but like diplomats, whose top hats and morning coats conceal a wariness, a maneuvering for position, a knowledge that an outburst of open anger might even be self-defeating if your opponent remained calm. We would have made poor material for a playwright.

We never had that big, long-postponed talk. We argued only about smaller things, usually some decision of mine about a summer job, or my choice of friends. The arguments were always polite and controlled, as if we were disagreeing over something in the morning's paper instead of over the course of my life. Thus there was no pivotal episode to our play, no catharsis, no release. Instead, I could cope with the pressure I felt from him only by putting thousands of miles between us. In the end I asserted my independence not by a scene of violent confrontation but by exiting from the stage.

I had been changed by that summer in South Africa—or perhaps it had just shaken into being a change that would have happened sooner or later in response to other events. For, when I returned to the United States, it was as if I could hear all around me echoes of my own new awareness. At college some of us organized the first student peace march on Washington. On the Boston Common I carried picket signs under the watchful eye of FBI agents. Friends departed on Freedom Rides to the South.

Standing in a huge, hushed crowd before the Lincoln Memorial, I heard Martin Luther King Jr.'s "I Have a Dream" speech. For the first time I had the feeling that I was living not just in a constricted life of my own but at a particular moment in history. The 1960s had begun.

In the summer of 1964, when I was twenty-one and a year out of college, I spent several weeks as a civil rights worker in Mississippi. It was not long enough to do anybody much good, but it was long enough to see that South Africa's injustices were mirrored closer to home. And its violence. I stayed in an old wooden house in a tree-shaded black neighborhood; in the evening carloads of young whites cruised by, screaming "Nigger lovers!" One night shortly after I left, the building, where other voter registration workers were still living, was torn open by a dynamite bomb.

In the fall of that year, I moved to San Francisco and went to work as a newspaper reporter. It was important to me to make my own way in the world, and not just financially. I still felt so defined by my connection with Father, with Eagle Nest, and with the wide network of friends and acquaintances and people who owed him favors that I could feel free only some distance away.

I had another reason, as well, for being drawn to California: the woman I was in love with was getting a graduate degree at Berkeley. I had met Arlie Russell a few years before, and had found with her a mutual warmth, passion, and understanding far greater than I had ever found with anyone else. But that is another story. Suffice it to say that without her I would never have been able to write this one.

Starting my job at the newspaper in San Francisco felt

like stepping into a new and wholly different world. I was first sent for several months to the press room at police headquarters. There, reporters for all the papers in town worked in shifts almost around the clock. We waited to see if anyone interesting got arrested, phoned the coroner periodically to see if there were any "jumpers" (off the Golden Gate Bridge), and listened to the police radio to keep track of crimes in progress.

A reporter from a rival paper offered me some friendly advice the first day I was there. He was an older man I will call Count Kelly, who had worked the police beat for thirty years and treated it as his own fief.

"Kid," the Count said, pointing at a wall map of San Francisco, "anything that happens *here* is news." With his finger he marked off the upper-right-hand corner of the city, which contained the wealthiest neighborhoods. "Anything anywhere else, unless it's really good—like a murder—you can forget. And black-on-black murders you don't have to bother about at all."

The Count believed the role of a newspaperman was to entertain. People wanted a good story, so why not give it to them?

"People like animals in their stories," he said. "If there isn't an animal in the story, you put it there. If the animal doesn't have a name, you give it one."

And, indeed, I noticed that in his paper, cats named Blackie, talking parrots, or faithful dogs named Max always were found drawing attention to the scene of a robbery or mourning beside the body of a dead master.

The Count added many other details to stories as well, whenever real-life events were not sufficiently exciting. Most of these would have to be agreed to in advance by the other reporters in the press room, so there would be no discrepancies among our various stories. Once, we were all listening in on extension phones and taking notes while the Count was on the line to a policeman who was at the scene of a burglary.

"How much did they take?" the Count asked.

"Three thousand in cash," the cop said.

The Count put his hand over the telephone mouthpiece and said to the rest of us in the press room, "Let's make that ten thousand in jewels, O.K., fellas?"

In San Francisco, to all appearances I make a splendid start to a new and independent life: a good job, a lovely fiancée, a small apartment we share on the edge of Chinatown, a commute to work on a cable car with a clanging bell. I casually stand on the running board, distinguished from all the camera-laden tourists by the tool of my trade, the reporter's notebook in my coat pocket. On my desk in those years the copper-ingot paperweights from Eagle Nest are nowhere in sight. Except for Arlie, no one here knows anything about my background; I am just another young person come to make a start in this most hospitable of cities. I take refuge in the anonymity of vagueness: "Where are you from?" "New York." As a reporter I chase fire engines, cover meetings at City Hall, question survivors of shipwrecks and airplane crashes, and am dispatched to the scene when a woman gives birth in a taxicab. This is, I tell myself exultantly, the real world at last. I even belong to a union.

One day a journalist from England comes to town. He calls and asks: "Can I interview you about California politics for a book I'm doing?"

I am delighted. I know the man's writing; he is South African by origin, but has lived many years in Britain. We go out to eat. He questions me at length about various state and local politicians, about what he should write about. He is witty and urbane, and takes notes in a neat, microscopic hand. This is the first time anyone has ever interviewed me. Can I really have become this expert? Are my words that valued by a fellow professional? He treats me to a good meal and I bask in enjoyment.

After dinner the woman who is with him, whom he apparently has met only a few days before, leaves us for a few minutes to go to the ladies' room. The journalist pushes aside his notebook and looks across the table at me:

"You're Harold Hochschild's son, right?"

I nod reluctantly, found out. So everything has been leading up to this.

"Well," he says, "I write for a living, but my real work is in the South African resistance." He names the organization. "I need to know if you have any information on what The Company's attitude will be if the World Court rules against South Africa on the Namibia question. That's important for us to know. What can you tell us about this?"

A few years later, I grow impatient with daily newspaper work and want to write more about the great social issues the whole country seems to be awakening to. I go to work for *Ramparts* magazine. It is zany but exciting. Assuming the office phones are tapped, we dash out to make key calls from pay phones. We junior staff writers work in cubicles with partitions that do not come all the way to the ceiling; sometimes I look up from my typewriter and see the hairy underside of a small monkey flying from partition to partition above my head. It is the office mascot, named Henry Luce.

I travel to Cuba, to the Kentucky coal country, and, undercover, to John Birch Society meetings in southern California. I interview student strikers, war resisters in military prisons, organizers in the slums of Chicago. I cover the street battles at the 1968 Democratic National Convention, where Mayor Daley's police charge at antiwar protesters with clubs swinging. Hesitantly at first, then with more confidence, I begin to feel part of a community: young journalists, activists, the generation of the sixties.

Sometimes, unexpectedly, this new life provides a view of the one I have come from. One day *Ramparts* sends me to Colorado to investigate a complicated scandal involving oil leases on Federal land. Again, the thrill of the real world: local people who have tried to expose these misdeeds have been threatened, even shot at; one lends me a pistol to keep in my rented room "just in case anything happens."

I try to act businesslike, as if this sort of thing happens to me every day. But I am secretly jubilant: could I ever be farther from the world of Eagle Nest? And can I be successfully pulling off such a feat here, in the state where, ironically, The Company has one of its largest mines? I happily pass as, merely, a reporter for a radical magazine. I have become good at passing.

On my last appointment before flying home to write the story, I interview an official of a state board that regulates mineral rights. He sits in an old, dusty office piled high with legal papers, in a cavernous stone building near the state capitol. He puffs on a cigar and leans back in his chair; he is about to retire, and no longer has any fear of talking about what he knows. He tells me what I need for my article, and then rambles on:

"But you know, you're on the wrong story, sonny. The

folks who *really* run this state aren't the oil boys; it's the people who own that big mine up at Climax. Why, they've got half the legislature in their pocket! Wouldn't pay their taxes. Claimed all the metal they were taking out of the ground up there had no value until it was re- fined in Pennsylvania or somewhere. We had to take 'em to court. They own this state! And I've seen the way those mining honchos live in New York, with their three- hour lunches and their fancy homes out in the sub- urbs. . . . "

My past and present lives seemed to clash most strongly during the several years I worked, in my mid- twenties, at *Ramparts*. It was a great thrill to be writing for the country's largest progressive magazine, which pe- riodically made headlines with its muckraking attacks on the Vietnam War. I was especially proud to have gotten the job there solely because of my newspaper reporting; no one at the magazine knew where I was from. A few months after I began working there, however, I was found out. Another writer on the staff had started re- searching American corporations in Africa. I knew it could be only a matter of time, and came to the office each morning in dread. One day, at last, he came across Father's name: "Hey, Adam, are you related to this guy?"

A short time later I worked, in a small way, on the most important exposé the magazine did—the disclosure that for many years the CIA had secretly financed dozens of supposedly private organizations involved in interna- tional affairs. The story caused an uproar in many coun- tries, and was on American front pages for a week. I felt borne along on a wave of excitement: each day TV crews arrived at the *Ramparts* office from Washington, New York, London. The whole world seemed to be paying attention to something I was doing. Newspapers competed with one another to unravel still further the web of CIA financial conduits we had exposed, and each day discovered more groups that were receiving this secret funding or had received it in the past.

Then, abruptly, as the news media continued investigating, the story took a twist that astonished me. One of these newly revealed former CIA fronts, whose actual funding had ceased only a few years before, turned out to be the African-American Institute. Father had been chairman of its board for a decade. The next time I saw him he seemed uncomfortable. He defended the link, saying that in its early years there was nowhere else the Institute could have gotten enough money for its work. But he was clearly embarrassed that the whole thing had had to be kept secret.

All these experiences made me redouble my efforts to separate myself from Father's way of life. When my parents visited me in San Francisco, Father always wanted to take me and some of my friends out to dinner at the fanciest restaurant in town. I clumsily searched for some excuse not to go. Each time he felt disappointed and hurt.

From my new perch in the world of Left journalism I also gradually came to learn a good deal more about the ways The Company had made its money. There turned out to be a great many things which had never been discussed over the Eagle Nest dinner table: a years-long protest against The Company's strip-mining in Appalachia; a storm of opposition from Indians in British Columbia, who said their ancestral fishing grounds were threatened by pollution from one of its mines; a long, fruitless attempt by Australian aborigines to try to stop a planned Company mine from desecrating land sacred to them. The meek may inherit the earth, J. Paul Getty once said, but they can forget about the mineral rights.

During my twenties, I began to notice the birth dates in newspaper obituaries: 1885. 1890. 1907. The dates bracketed Father's own, 1892, and I found myself wondering when his own time would be up. Would that free me from his disapproval?

The same pattern that lay behind those sessions in his study after lunch, when I had done something he thought wrong the day before, continued as I grew up. Although Father prided himself on not automatically expecting me to go to work for The Company (as *his* father had made *him* do), he nonetheless had a fairly clear idea of what I should do with my life. This unwritten plan he never laid out directly, but it became all too visible, bit by bit, as I departed from it. With each such step, he became more disturbed.

In his life plan, I was to go to Yale (where he had gone), then to law school (which he wished he had done), then work in one of the big New York law firms for a few years, preferably dealing with international matters. Then I would go to work as an aide to a bright, young, rising—and, of course, WASP—politician, such as New York's Mayor John Lindsay, whom Father much admired. And then (as Father had realized in retrospect he would have liked to do) I would go farther into the political world, maybe as something like an Assistant Secretary of State, appointed when my mentor reached higher office. I would make a variety of friends, but most would be from old New York and New England Social Register families, people who had "breeding"—a word Father used often. During this time, of course, there would be Eagle Nest in the summers, with my wife (who would have no work of her own, of course) and children spending the entire summer there while I commuted on weekends, solving the problems of the world in New York or Washington during the week.

My course diverged from this scenario rather rapidly. And at each of my turning points, at each major decision, came a frown of disapproval from Father, a cloud which never quite dissipated, but which lingered for years in small questions and reminders: "Your novel, Adam, when will it be *finished*?"

Father was accustomed to seeing things done his way: he held enough power in the world so that direct orders from him to others were often not necessary; dropped hints were enough. But now, someone was not following those hints, and that disconcerted him deeply.

Paradoxically, for he was an excellent stylist himself and had read Kipling and Dickens aloud to me when I was a boy, he was particularly opposed to my being a writer. Because, he thought, I risked becoming a "dilet-tante"—something of which Father seemed to have an almost obsessive fear. Writers had some minor utility, to his way of thinking; they produced commodities he con-sumed: Broadway plays, history books, an occasional novel or biography. But unless they were columnists for the *Times,* they were clearly secondary to the real work of the world. If you did it at all, writing was something to be done after your real work was done, on evenings and weekends—which was when he had worked on his own Adirondack history book.

What had previously been a summons to Father's study now became a flight by him to the West Coast. Os-tensibly it was for a social visit to Arlie and me—we had gotten married after I had been in California for a year.

But his real purpose was to tell me at some length, very articulately, that whatever was my most recent decision was a mistake, a really quite major mistake, with serious long-range consequences I wasn't aware of. That was his response no matter what my decision: to live in San Francisco, to get married, to stay in journalism, to write a book, to work for *Ramparts,* to leave *Ramparts* and start a new magazine.

I usually knew before each visit which aspect of my life was on his agenda. I steeled myself for the moment when that point would be raised. Perhaps it would come at the end of dinner on our second evening together—when Father figured that enough time had passed so that it would not look as if voicing disapproval had been the main purpose of his visit.

He always first went through the motions of inquiring about what I was doing:

"And how are things at the magazine, Adam?"

"Pretty good. We've got some great pieces lined up for the next issue."

But he didn't really want to hear, and his perfunctory replies always came too quickly: "Yes . . . yes . . . I see . . . Oh that's interesting . . . yes, isn't that interesting."

Then he would clear his throat nervously and begin:

"There's something I've been meaning to talk to you about, Adam. You're a good writer; that last article was really very good. But there are some things I think you'd be still *better* at. And I'm concerned that you may be wasting your real talent by avoiding them."

If these arguments between us took place when my mother was present, she was always anxious. Sometimes she found an excuse to leave the room. Sometimes she would afterward repeat Father's opinion in a way that gave it a softer edge: "I think Father's only concerned, dear, that you don't hurt your own career by what you're doing. You know he wants only the best for you."

As always, she never disagreed with him. And, I started to realize now, that pattern had added greatly to my self-doubt, to my childhood sense that I *was* in fact guilty of whatever Father accused me of. Why did she, someone who loved me so much in every other way, whose love was always so supportive, so unconditional, not stand by me here? Why didn't she stop him? *Why?* Beneath her genuine love for him, I began to see, she must have been afraid of Father's wrath as well.

I had no conflict with my mother directly. She cared only that I loved my wife and my work, and—especially—that we planned to have children. For her, that was enough, and she was happy. I could not really talk with her about the books I read or the ones I wanted to write. But about my writing, which so greatly aggravated Father, she said, "Most people never really find a way out of themselves. It looks as if you have."

As she grew older, the two sides of her I had always known seemed more in contrast than ever. Her hypochondria grew worse: she went to doctors frequently, talked about her problems with her eyes, her sinuses, her back, and developed new ailments if old ones were cured. When traveling or on public occasions she often asked for a wheelchair, as if to confirm her status as an invalid. At Eagle Nest, all her possessions seemed to be precautionary: sleep shades against the light; candles against the dark, in case the electricity went off; wool face masks against the winter cold, though she stepped outside only for a few seconds between house and car.

Medicines against all sorts of ills kept surfacing around the house, like stones yielded up by a field.

Yet this same woman who could fret aloud for days about whether she would be quite comfortable enough at Montego Bay, or whether the trip would be just too much for her, never lost her ability to sympathize with the underdog. She showered friendly advice on friends in trouble, and was a sympathetic listener when they wanted to confide in her. She found people psychiatrists, prospective mates, summer jobs, places to live. When an old friend died, she took the woman's teenage son to live with her and Father for three months.

And, despite a life of being waited on, her empathy stretched well beyond her own class. I began to see that it was from her that I had first picked up certain basic beliefs I had always taken for granted: that black people in the United States had a raw deal; that labor unions were a good thing; that most wars were pointless. Once, when I was pushing her in her wheelchair to a college commencement ceremony where Father was to get an honorary degree, she burst into tears at the thought that some of the young men in the audience might be killed, senselessly, in Vietnam.

When Father's attempts to dissuade me from my alleged mistake of the moment were unsuccessful, as they always were, he resorted to the mail. These particular letters, many pages of argument closely typed, or handwritten on long, yellow paper, as carefully thought out as lawyers' briefs, were heralded by their legal-size envelopes, and my stomach tightened whenever I saw them.

Unlike the usual parent-child arguments of the Viet-

nam era, my political differences with Father were less
of substance than of style. Father considered himself a
liberal Democrat, and talked about "my friend Norman
Thomas" in the same way white liberals used to boast
about having black friends. But there are worse sins. He
had hated Joe McCarthy, and had friends among Mc-
Carthy's victims. And from the very start, Father was totally opposed to the war in Vietnam. But he believed that
the way you changed things was by writing letters to *The
New York Times,* by running for office, and by reasoning
quietly with your friends, who, of course, were people of
influence.

Why doesn't Adam *see*? he must have thought, exasperated and impatient: that boy could have everything.
He's been to the right schools. He's got the right connections. We gave him everything. All doors are open to
him. Things *I* couldn't have done because my father
made me go into The Company. But he could be a con-
gressman, senator, ambassador, work for the Ford Foundation if he doesn't like business or law, do something
that *counts*. What's wrong with him? He's got some sort
of neurosis. He's running away from something. All this
damnfoolery of living in California and working for some
magazine nobody's ever heard of. If he wants to change
the world, why not get into some position where he'll
have the power to do something? If he goes on this way,
he'll reach a point where he can't turn back anymore—
even if he comes to his senses and wants to.

During this first decade I am away from home, I find that
even though those outbursts of Father's disapproval may
come only once or twice a year, their shadow is always
in the background, as if he will appear before me at any

moment to argue that whatever I'm doing is not really worthwhile. The Russians are right to use patronymics, for truly, it seems, I will be Adam, son of Harold, all life long. I am always wary of him.

I call home fairly frequently, for I'm a conscientious son, the sort who remembers birthdays and answers letters. But I know my parents' Eagle Nest routine: the hour of the swim, the ride, the waterskiing, and I always call at times when he is likely to be out, so I will be able to talk just to my mother.

Once I calculate wrong and he answers. "Oh Adam! How are you? I'm so glad you called! We were just talking about you."

He sounds genuinely happy to hear my voice. This surprises me. I don't know what to say. Is he really glad to hear from me? Has he been thinking of me fondly, after all? I wonder about this, as the days go by. But I am not able to admit that this could be so. Not yet.

XVI

Once, for the first time as an adult, I reread the history book about the central Adirondacks Father wrote in his spare time some twenty years earlier. I am stunned by how good it is: how gracefully written, how vivid its portraits of people, and how wide-angled its social sweep: from the robber barons who built huge summer homes in the 1890s to hermits who lived in the forests in winter. It honors the lives of ordinary people normally invisible to summer visitors: lumberjacks, trappers, railwaymen. All these are the very qualities I had come—independently, I thought—to admire in good writing. I resolve to tell him how much I like the book, the next time I see him. But that time comes and goes, as does another, and another, and I cannot bring myself to tell him.

Hardly anyone else seems to see that judgmental side of Father. It is as if there are two different relationships between him and me. One is a chipper, upbeat friendship, with a certain amount of joking and sharing of family news and memories of things done together in the past. There are some happy moments. And, I have to admit, my guard goes down at such times, and I feel something approaching love. When he comes for a visit, Father brings me some old photos or an article he knows I'll want to read. Others observe this and no doubt think: a boy who gets on well with his father, unlike so many youngsters these days. . . . The other is a relationship filled with unease and apprehension. I always store up a supply of extraneous, time-filling things to say when I know I will be having a long meal or a drive alone with him, to fend off the silence which might turn into a new voicing of his disapproval. Or, worse, into that conversation we have never had, unbearably intimate, about the two of us. The conversation which might begin—I dread this most of all—by his asking me to call him something other than the absurdly formal "Father."

Only Arlie can also see both sides. For the first time I am no longer alone with my perceptions. Once we visit Eagle Nest for a week soon after we are married, and Arlie goes riding with Father. They go through the woods to the old airplane hangar on the lake shore. Father is riding a new horse, which is scared of wading into the shallow water; it balks. But Father is determined, as a matter of principle, that the horse put its feet in the water. For ten minutes the horse refuses, pirouettes, rears and neighs in protest. For ten minutes Father kicks with his spurs, speaks sternly, whacks the horse's rump with a leather crop. Finally, the horse steps into the water.

Later Arlie tells me: "Now I understand."

Sometimes Father tests my own balkiness. He bargains hard over the dates of our summer visits to Eagle Nest, always wanting them to be longer, never giving up the hope that we will spend the whole summer there, instead of just a week or so. He calls me in California; there is a faint babble of other voices on the line, as if somewhere between us a thousand fathers are talking to a thousand sons.

"What day are you arriving, Adam?"

"We're coming around the seventh."

"Oh, make it a few days earlier," he replies. "If you're here on the fifth, then S—— will still be here for the weekend, and you know how much he'll want to see you."

"No, I don't think we can come that early."

A week or two later he calls again: "So you're coming on the fifth, right?"

If I say no, the seventh, he will pout; if I say yes, the fifth, I will be giving in. There is no way out.

And at other times there are yet more knots. Another argument about my life, for example, which ends with him saying: "Remember [translation: Be *grateful*], I didn't make you go to Yale or into The Company." A pause for the final twist: " . . . And I'm not so sure that was a good thing."

I have sometimes wondered: Am I telling the truth about Father? My own apprehensiveness toward him, my dread of being alone with him, is so much at odds with the image of the wise, generous man remembered by his friends.

Once, recently, I sought out a former visitor to Eagle Nest whom I hadn't seen for several decades. I asked him what he recalled about Father in the years when I was small—was I now skewed in my memory of him, focusing on those reprimands I used to get for talking too much?

No, the man said; he remembered one such time,

when, as we were all sitting on the great flagstone porch of the Club House and I was about seven, he saw Father turn on me angrily for some totally innocuous remark, and say: "Don't *ever* say anything like that again."

"Did I cry? What was my reaction?" I asked, suddenly understanding that *that* was the important question.

"Silence," said the man, "complete silence."

And that, I think, is how I got back at Father. Effectively. Not just as a small child, but as an adult, too. I withdrew. With a determination, and a politeness, that rivaled his own. I was a dutiful son, but not a fully loving one, and eventually the dutifulness—writing home once a week, sending thank-you notes, remembering what food he liked when he visited us in California—added up to a kind of ironic substitute for a deeper love that for a long time I withheld.

The withholding was always in small ways. When he came to see us on the West Coast, he always anxiously tried to set the date of his next visit; I tried to put it off. There was always a politics of dates between us.

"I thought I'd come for the weekend of the fourteenth, next month," he would say, pulling out his appointment book. "Would that be O.K.?"

"Well . . . I think we have something going on that weekend," I would reply. "What about the one of the twenty-first? Or the twenty-eighth—that would be even better."

When Arlie and I came to Eagle Nest, I went through the right gestures, even Getting The Beer. But I tended to come a little late and leave a little early from the cocktails/dinner/after-dinner-coffee routine of the Club House, as if to say: I'm going through the motions, but I don't really belong here. What I think he wanted above all, and never got, was that sense that I did belong there, liked being there, felt relaxed and comfortable there, appreciated the world he had created. He wanted me to come all the way home.

I had graduated from college when there was still a draft; to avoid it, I entered the Army Reserve. I spent several surprisingly enjoyable months on active duty, mostly driving trucks and building outhouses at Fort Devens, Massachusetts. A few years later, in San Francisco, I was still going to my required weekly Reserve drills when large numbers of U.S. combat troops began going to Vietnam. I organized a national group of antiwar Reservists and National Guardsmen. Several thousand of us signed a statement calling for the immediate withdrawal of all American troops. Father was horrified. Writing letters to the editor was one thing, but inciting soldiers to sign a protest was quite another.

Father was not upset because he thought what I was doing was wrong but because he thought it might get me branded as an outcast. It would be sure to cause major problems with my getting jobs, with my ever going into politics, and so forth: "Adam, you're right about the war, but you just don't realize: this will be on your *record.*" In one of these arguments he quoted some German proverb whose point was that you should not unnecessarily rock the boat. I heard an undertone from the past: his fear for me was a very Jewish fear.

Several months later, our Reservists' group filed a lawsuit, which was judged important on constitutional grounds and eventually wound up in the Supreme Court. The suit was not only reported prominently in the *Times,* but because the reporter had accidentally left some information out of the first story, it appeared in the paper two days running. Father's entire attitude toward this project changed, and from then on he always asked respectfully about our activities. For once I felt triumphant.

XVII

For Boris's eightieth birthday there was a big party: dinner, toasts with champagne, waltzing. Boris had recently had an operation to implant an electronic pacemaker for his heart, and he showed it off to people between dances. His cheerful directness was unchanged. "It's good," he told me, proudly tapping the metallic bulge beneath his shirt. "It will give me another two or three years." He was exactly right.

When I was a child, I loved Boris, but when I moved away from home, I suppressed some of that feeling. During my twenties it was more comfortable to think of him merely as a *Reader's Digest* "Unforgettable Character," an exotic figure from an old home movie, colorful but no longer relevant. How could I, a 1960s radical with Cuban posters on my wall, admit that someone who meant so much to me still had two pictures of Tsar Nicholas II on his?

It wasn't until the last year or so of Boris's life, when I was nearing thirty, that I came to feel differently. I found myself thinking about him more and more. He lived in the present; he enjoyed life to the full; he repressed nothing. Of how many people could I say that? Certainly not of myself.

As an act of homage to Boris, or to that part of him I

wanted in my own life, I learned to fly a glider. There is something transcendent about this experience: you navigate in three dimensions among invisible fountains and waterfalls of air; you are at one with the birds. I wrote to him about that, the first letter I'd ever written him. He wrote back a beautiful note in the handwriting of Russian émigrés: many curls on the letters, and false starts where Cyrillic characters had been reluctantly converted in mid-stroke to Roman ones. He said that he, too, had flown gliders and appreciated "the beauty and the silence," although perhaps someday I would learn to fly power planes also: then I would no longer be bounded by the air currents, and the whole world would be mine.

On a visit to Eagle Nest a few months later, I went to see him and Gertrude. We had just had our first child, and Boris grunted with satisfaction as he watched Arlie nurse the baby "just like we used to in Russia." As with wontons and ravioli and many other things, he seemed about to claim that Russians had invented breast-feeding.

Then he and I went off to a corner. Boris's frame was as broad as ever, but he moved very slowly now. We talked for an hour or so, probably the only time we had talked alone for so long. We both knew it would be the last. It was then that he told me the whole story of his life, which up to now I had heard only in fragments from others. He talked about growing up in Russia; about learning to fly; about the wars he had fought; and about the great battle in 1919 when the White Army almost recaptured Petrograd. "We were so close. We were so close, Adam, I could see the golden towers of St. Peter and St. Paul."

But then Trotsky arrived in Petrograd in his famous

armored train, rallied the Reds, and the army Boris was with had to retreat. On that day the tide of war turned and it was clear that the Tsar's Russia was gone forever.

"There was much dying. I was one of the lucky ones," Boris said. Outside the window, through the balsam trees, the sun turned the rippled surface of the lake into a sheet of silver. "I have had a good life. I have no regrets."

A few weeks after that last conversation with Boris, I sent him a picture a friend had taken of me flying a glider. When there was no letter in return, I knew he was dying. I woke one morning and realized that I would never again stand on the lake shore, feel the propeller-blown spray on my face, and watch the Mallard thunder across the water and into the sky. I think it was at that moment that I first felt what age is, what death is.

In some ways Boris was easier to admire at a distance than close up. Maybe Gertrude was right never to talk politics. An ardent monarchist whose main political activity had consisted of shooting as many Reds as he could get in his gun sights, Boris would have cared nothing for the distinctions—so vital to me—between the Communist and non-Communist Left. He was probably unaware of my own politics. If he had known about them, and if I had been his son, he would have disowned me.

Only after Boris's death did I learn how tempestuous had been his relationship with his own son. Boris had been married twice before he met Gertrude, and from the first marriage, in Russia, he had a boy. War and revolution separated the two for more than a decade. After much hardship, Orest Sergievsky managed to make his way out of the Soviet Union in the late 1920s. From occasional Eagle Nest summer weekends when I was a boy, I remembered his expressive face, his exuberance. A professional dancer, he had a strong, barrel-chested torso developed from years of hoisting ballerinas aloft.

In an age when it was far more difficult to be open about it than it is today, Orest was a homosexual. And his great passion in life was ballet. It was not clear which of the two things galled Boris more, but he focused his vehement disapproval on Orest's dancing.

"There was a war between [my] father and myself all the time," Orest said in an interview with a dance magazine some years after Boris had died. " . . . He absolutely hated the idea of my dancing. He was ashamed of it, and never told anyone about it. . . . It was a terrible time." Boris demanded that Orest take a job as a riveter at the Sikorsky aircraft factory, something Boris thought more manly than dancing.

"We were both interested in ballerinas," Orest once told me sadly, "but for different reasons."

Despite fierce opposition from Boris, Orest had a successful career in ballet. He danced with the Metropolitan Opera Ballet and other companies; when he retired from performing, he started his own dance company and teaching studio, and was a guest teacher in many others. He and his father finally made a truce of sorts. But Boris's dismay never disappeared. When Orest was dancing professionally, Boris said to him once, "You mean people actually *pay* to see you?"

Maybe I was better off with Father after all.

A few days after Boris's death, hundreds of his friends gathered for his funeral at a Russian Orthodox Church in New York, where the soul of this quite unreligious man was sent on its way amid incense, icons, flickering candles, and chanting, black-bearded priests. The next day Gertrude, with great emotion, gave me Boris's watch, which I still wear: a large, sturdy aviator's watch with an extra hand that shows Greenwich Mean Time, the time which airplanes fly by.

In the days that followed, there again seemed to be the promise of an opening to Gertrude, a chance to talk to her at last. For she wanted to publish a memorial book about Boris, and asked my help in finding out about type-setters and printers. But after I had sent her some information and had heard nothing, I asked her about the project again and she changed the subject.

In her quiet way, Gertrude had the same force of character as her brother, Father. When she changed the subject, you did not change it back. Mysteriously, all discussion of Boris with her had now become taboo. It was only some years later that I learned the likely reason: this was the point at which Gertrude had discovered that in his will Boris had left much of the money she had given him over the years to many of his former mistresses.

Gertrude herself survived Boris by only a few years. But it seems that at the very end, with what must have taken considerable generosity of spirit, she forgave him. For she left instructions that her ashes were to be scattered over the lake at Eagle Nest—from an airplane.

XVIII

On one occasion when I was about thirty, at the time of year when, as a boy, I would have gone to Eagle Nest for the summer, I found myself spending the night in a hotel in southern California. The rooms were white: white rugs, white telephones, ghost-white bedspreads and lampshades. There were walls of mirror, a constant freeway hum in the background, a man in a sports shirt in the lobby selling real estate. On a hill nearby were wavelike rows of condominiums, and on the next range of hills, bulldozers were gouging out space for more.

Waking in the morning, seeing myself in all this whiteness in the mirror-wall, I suddenly missed the warm look and rough feel of the wooden walls in my bedroom and all the rooms of Eagle Nest, the sound of the wind in the pine trees, the ripple of waves on the lake shore. This feeling took me by surprise. It was all wrong, said my social conscience, honed to querulous sharpness by nearly a decade on the leftward edges of political journalism. Indulgence! Class privilege! We lived at that time in a two-room apartment in Berkeley, close to the campus where Arlie taught; I prided myself on not being attached to material things. If cinder-block-and-plywood desks and a VW bug were good enough for our friends, they were good enough for us. I knew, of course, I would never live on that Adirondack estate in the style my parents did, but now the question occurred to me: Was it still, in some deeper sense that did not have to do with living there, my home?

A year or two later, I am on a visit back East to see my parents, now in their seventies. It is June; I accompany them as they go to Eagle Nest for the summer. As is often the case now, my mother is ill with some vague psychosomatic malady; to spare her the long drive, Father has chartered a plane, so we approach Eagle Nest from the air, as in the old days. The last wooded ridge falls away beneath us; the plane banks to land on the lake; the houses are lined up in their accustomed places along the shore, which I know to the inch. Seeing it from the air, from the perspective of the mapmaker, I feel overwhelmed with a feeling of *possession*. At first I am dismayed, for this is not the emotion I want to have. But, going over it in bed that night, I realize that my feeling is not one of possession in the sense of wanting to protect something that is mine, to be defended against others, but of possession as you possess your own past, which belongs to no one else, and whose power over you must be admitted, felt, accepted, before you can leave it behind and live the life before you.

There have been many returns to Eagle Nest, many homecomings over the years. Homecomings by train, when the railroad still ran, leaving Grand Central Station at night, the train loaded with bundles of the old *New York Herald Tribune,* which were put on board fresh from the press at the last minute; then the feeling of mystery and adventure as I awoke rolling through an evergreen forest at dawn, woods so deep that some small towns in them could not be reached by road, only by train. Then the familiar stop where the Eagle Nest station wagon was waiting, exhaust pipe puffing a comforting white cloud into the cold morning air. Homecomings from the sky with Boris, when we roared over the waving cluster of people on the lake shore and touched down in a splash of spray. Homecomings in an old airport limousine we called "the bus," which held a dozen people, where I squirmed restlessly in my seat while my mother fed me popcorn or cookies from her handbag and Father told me to stop talking so much. And then, much later, when both of them are dead, there will be homecomings alone, in a car rented at the nearest airport, as if I am a traveler going somewhere, rather than returning.

Eagle Nest—the old Eagle Nest, the place where it was always summer, the province of Old Russia adrift in time—lasted for me from 1945, when Father and Boris came home from the war, to about ten years later, when Gertrude moved her family to a separate house. From Hiroshima to Suez, in fact; the decade when America most confidently ruled the world. After that the place began to change, although it was as if I awoke to these changes slowly, only long after they had happened.

Christmas 1974. Arlie and I visit for the holidays, staying at the Cottage; there are no guests at the Club House, although, as they have done for the last half-century, the "help" have cut a giant Christmas tree in the woods, brought it in, and decorated it with all the old ornaments and tinsel and lights. It seems smaller than the trees we had when I was a child, though it reaches the ceiling. A Christmas card tells us that Colonel Natirboff, now long retired from the stables, is dying in a hospital in Miami. I make the ritual visits to the other family houses on the property. Snow on the tree branches which a few days ago was melting in the sun has been frozen by a cold snap into brilliantly shimmering filigrees of ice. The air is cheek-smarting, hand-numbing cold. My fingers and toes chill more swiftly than before. On all the buildings there are spear-curtains of icicles.

On the next lake, a villager's snowmobile scoots across the surface, a plume of dry, powdery snow rising behind it. Its driver is checking baited fishing lines hanging through holes chain-sawed in the ice. On a few back porches in town nearby, sides of venison from the fall hunting season hang in the freezing air. All these things which I once thought a romantic part of life in the north woods appear in a different light now, as I talk with people from the town. In the winter there are few jobs here. People hunt because they can't afford beef. They saw fishing holes through thirty inches of ice not for sport but for food. Those wonderful stocky draft horses, with their long manes and their breath steaming in the winter air, are now sometimes used for logging once again, as they were in my childhood, not because they are picturesque but because hay costs less than diesel fuel. When the local timber companies lay people off by the score, there are several suicides. Can all this be the setting of my childhood summer paradise? The surrounding world here has darker colors now; the old Eagle Nest seems not just a place but a state of mind.

XIX

When Boris died, Father was long retired. He was abroad, having taken half a dozen friends with him as his guests; they were in Afghanistan when he got a telegram with the news of Boris's death. Leaving his friends to continue their itinerary, Father flew back to New York for a day and a half. During that time he twice went to call on Gertrude at her apartment, staying half an hour or so each time.

"How was it?" I asked.

"Well," he said, "Gertrude and I have often had a hard time talking to each other."

Then he flew back, halfway around the world, to resume his trip.

Just as Father had married late, when he was nearly fifty, so too did one of his greatest achievements come late, when he was nearly eighty. For the last half of his life, his great avocation was the Adirondack Mountains. He wrote his history book, founded a museum, and served on boards having to do with state historic sites and the like. The culmination of this mini-career came when he was appointed chairman of a New York State commission to make recommendations about the future of the

Adirondacks, which form the country's largest state or national park.

By appointing a group to study this question, Governor Rockefeller had mainly wanted to be able to get various pressure groups off his back. But in choosing Father, he got far more than he had bargained for. Under Father's direction, the commission drafted the country's toughest package of regional conservation laws, which would protect the forest and make further real estate development extremely difficult. Environmentalists everywhere hailed this program; Father was celebrated with awards, newspaper editorials, honorary degrees. Often, after dinner on an Eagle Nest weekend, while a houseful of guests sat over coffee in front of the big fireplace, someone would ask him about the work of his commission. As he started to explain, the whole room would fall respectfully silent.

But the battle was not yet over; the recommendations of Father's commission still had to be turned into law by the state legislature. Fierce lobbying by developers stalled the bill until the final night of the year's legislative session. At 2 a.m., Father, who had been watching everything from the gallery, asked to see the Speaker of the State Assembly.

"If you make any more concessions to the real estate lobby," Father told the Speaker, "I'm going to call a press conference and say that our commission's recommendations have been betrayed." Father knew that there was an election coming and that both parties were courting the environmentalist vote.

I was not there, but I can so well imagine the scene in the Speaker's office: Father's voice was doubtless calm, not raised; polite, deliberate; his words precise and carefully chosen. The Speaker was weary and intimidated.

The Speaker gave in. The bill Father wanted was passed a few minutes later. A friend then drove Father from the state capitol at Albany back to New York City. He slept most of the way, except to wake once at dawn and remark:

"I liked the expression on the Speaker's face when he said, 'All right, you win, Mr. Hochschild.' "

A few years after this, while my parents were on a trip abroad, my mother had a cerebral hemorrhage. When Father called to tell me, it was the only time I had ever heard him sobbing. "She's in a coma, Adam. It's all over."

She was eight years younger than Father, and had always thought he would die first. So had I, because I could imagine being alone with her far more easily than I could with him. But now, in a fraction of a second, she had lost consciousness for good, unable to resort to the arsenal of pills she carried with her on all trips in a brown leather handbag.

I had always had a premonition that one or the other of them would die in a foreign country. Even though I traveled seldom at that point in my life, I kept my passport up-to-date. Father's call came in the middle of the night, from the Canary Islands, off the coast of Africa. I was on a plane a few hours later.

Despite being grown and married, thirty-one years old, I am afraid of being alone with him: my great, unspeakable childhood fear. She has been an intermediary between us, wanting so hard to make us love each other, repeating to me anything complimentary that she has heard him say about me, doubtless repeating to him anything of the sort she has heard from me. And doubtless embellishing in both directions, wishing that each of us had said more. She has shuttled between us like a peace envoy to the Middle East. But now, at last, the two of us are alone with each other.

They have been staying in a luxury hotel, of course, a big place with huge, elaborately carved wooden doors, and uniformed bellboys with little caps. My mother is unconscious, her brain drowned in blood. So we do not wait at her hospital bedside, but at the hotel. When the news comes of her actual, medical death, we are eating in the dining room, where an orchestra is playing dinner music.

We go to the hospital right away. Her eyes are closed; her hands lie limp on the sheet beside her. Father does not want to touch her, to feel her lifelessness with his hands. He stands at the door of the hospital room. I go closer, but still feel constrained by his example; I do not touch her either. How is it that I can fly across six thousand miles of continent and ocean, yet not walk the whole way across a room to touch someone I love? Even today, there still seems something incomplete about her death. I did not say good-bye, even if it was a good-bye she could not have heard.

Father does not want to eat in the hotel dining room again. And so the next night and the next and the next we eat at a restaurant nearby called the "Acuario," where the walls are tanks of tropical fish: huge turtles, eels, and fish with long spiky fins and brilliantly colored skin, who come at you, eyes bulging, then swerve away from the glass at the last moment. Afraid, perhaps, that he will break down in this public place, Father talks about arrangements for our travel back to the United States, about the Spanish islands where we are, about world politics.

Getting a dead body from one country to another turns

out to be immensely complicated: there are death certif-
icates to be signed, permissions to be granted, consuls to
be consulted. And so we stay on at the hotel for a week.
In a strange way, dealing with the slow-moving local bu-
reaucracy unites us, and we joke about how there always
turns out to be one more official stamp we need. Father
seems almost reluctant for the process to end, for he
dreads the crush of friends and relatives who will be
waiting to surround us at home, offering sympathy, hugs,
emotion, which all demand a display of feelings in return
from him.

Each night we eat together at the restaurant of the
tropical fish. When I am not getting officials to sign papers, I keep Father company in his relentless tourism,
seeing the island from the back of a limousine. Still uncomfortable with more intimate talk, each day we wake
and ask each other: "Did you sleep well?"

Once I venture, hesitantly: "I'm afraid it will be hard
for you . . . these next few months."

"I can manage," he says. "I had fifty years of being
alone."

After we come back to the United States, her body be-
comes smoke in the air near the Lincoln Tunnel; her
ashes are buried at the town cemetery near Eagle Nest, a
clearing in the woods under a mountain's brow. A minister is imported from New York to say a few words at
the burial, not because either of my parents was religious
but because, Father says, "the local people might be offended if we didn't have one." Various of them who
come to the short graveside ceremony doubtless do so
because they think *he* will be offended if they don't,
while he, embarrassed by all ceremony, probably would
prefer nothing at all, just as he never wants birthday
presents.

It was winter when she died, and so we receive letters and telegrams and messages from Florida, the Bahamas, radiograms from cruise ships afloat. Former servants send printed cards and announcements of masses to be said for her soul. From friends come letters on monogrammed stationery and notes on corporate letterhead, or messages, bracketed by long strings of numbers, that arrive on the telex machine at Company headquarters from all over the world.

XX

As Father entered his eighties, he began to loosen up somewhat, and that in turn loosened the tension between us. In more than thirty years of marriage, my mother had slowly begun to soften and mellow him. Now that she was gone, it was as if he were partly able to express what she had always expressed for them both.

Before, when he had called Arlie and me, it was usually to ask at first about some specific thing: "Did you get my letter of the nineteenth?" "Are you still arriving on the twenty-seventh?" But now sometimes he would call, talk about the weather, ask how we were; I would wait, guarded, suspicious, wondering what spark of disapproval or reminder of an obligation was coming; only after he hung up would I see that he had called just to talk. I would feel badly, regretting that I had not been more friendly. Sometimes, amazingly, he even called to ask my advice.

Once he wrote briefly but movingly that he missed my mother greatly. For a time after she died, he said, he felt she was still there, listening to things he heard, laughing with him at jokes people made. Now, her presence had ebbed away. It was one of the rare times he had written of his feelings. I wrote him back; he replied warmly. Throughout this time we were telephoning each other almost daily because of a series of arrangements about his next visit to San Francisco—yet when we talked on the phone or saw each other the next week he never mentioned anything about what was in the letters.

After my mother died, Father paused in his life for a few months, depressed and doing little. Then it was as if he looked around and decided to live a good while longer. He again began controlling his weight with the appalling diet he had followed for much of his life, several days a week consuming nothing but prunes, black coffee, and thick steak, rare or raw. He drank as much vodka as ever. On the stereo, he played John Philip Sousa marches, a favorite reminder of his World War II days. He resumed a unique practice he had followed for years: he believed that because of differences in air pressure you could flush a head cold out of your system by taking a short airplane flight. And for him, this seemed to work.

In earlier years, Father's sense of humor had often seemed hidden behind his solemnity. Now it flourished more in the open, visible especially in the humorous poetry he wrote and read aloud at black-tie celebrations of friends' birthdays and anniversaries. One poem was for the seventieth birthday of my mother's sister Sarnia, a saintly, timid, deeply religious woman who lived modestly in a one-room apartment and devoted herself to charitable work. Father catalogued all sorts of imaginary debauchery and high living by her, and ended:

> Such is the life that's been your norm;
> Now, at the seventies' gate,
> Oh, Sarnia, repent, reform,
> Before it is too late!

He wrote long, witty letters to friends about the state of the world, and he let no letter go unanswered. While the steam heat hissed and gurgled around the house unevenly, he spent long hours hunched over his typewriter in his Eagle Nest study. His feet were warmed by a multitude of heaters and heating pads; on the desk in front of him was a clutter of mail and a file marked ACKNOWLEDGED.

Father continued his practice of prodigiously showering gifts and invitations on people, although he seemed to do so with a more relaxed spirit than before. This habit born of some deep and mysterious anxiety had now partly, at least, become an enjoyable hobby. On Eagle Nest weekends, every guest room in the Club House was full. He took groups of six or eight friends with him when he went abroad. He went from Moscow to Khabarovsk on the Trans-Siberian Railroad. In India at the age of eighty-six, he rode a camel for the first time. He began giving away sums of money each year, to near and distant relatives, and to friends, particularly younger friends. He always gave because he liked somebody, generally not (although he did respond generously when people were in trouble) because a person needed the money. For this annual practice he even used his own term: "making a distribution." This was bewildering to the uninitiated, for usually a cryptic note, "This is part of a distribution I'm making," was the only message accompanying a check.

Although my parents had gone there at Christmas and for a few winter weekends, Eagle Nest had been mainly a summer home. But after my mother died, Father settled there permanently. He swam across the lake each summer evening, measuring the water temperature every time. He rode his horse daily the whole year. The weekend house parties went on year-round. After Rex died, Father got another yellow Labrador, feeding him, taking him to the vet, sharing between-meal snacks of raw steak with him, and going for walks and rides "because Nick needs some exercise." Could this be the man from my childhood, who for the first five years I had Rex wouldn't even allow him in the house?

He remained "Mr. Harold" to the local people. There was not just feudalism in those words but respect and a certain awe as well—no other summer families rated that form of address. Townspeople came up and shook his hand when he appeared at the local general store. Bizarrely, it must have seemed to these villagers, it was this Jewish industrialist from the big city who had made himself the leading expert on central Adirondack history. What had drawn him to this subject? Not introspective, he never speculated; the rest of us never really knew. For his book, he had interviewed dozens of old-timers: steamboat hands, wilderness guides, French-Canadian woodsmen. The museum of Adirondack life he founded won national recognition. He knew as much as anyone alive about the tools and camp life of the nineteenth-century lumberjacks who cut down the big trees by hand, before the days of tractors and chain saws. History journals sent him books on the subject to review.

And, stranger still, his neighbors must have thought, in this region where summer residents depart on Labor Day and where even local retired people who can scrape together enough money head for Florida for the winter, this man in his eighties had decided to live year-round. In particularly cold weather, when nighttime temperatures dropped to minus forty degrees Fahrenheit and the sap froze and tree trunks cracked like rifle shots, he simply added a cloth hood and face mask to the red parka and fur mittens he wore while riding.

Although it seemed as if he would live forever, Father planned for his own death in the same methodical way in which he planned for everything. He threw out old files, reorganized others, and sorted through fifty years of date books and records. Among them he found some diary entries about some of the weekend trips he and I had made together when I was small. He copied out several of these and sent them to me, in a gesture meant to recall good times spent together. For me it was bittersweet. I had to admit now that he had been trying to reach out to me with those trips, a man then in his late fifties, inexperienced at fatherhood, searching for something that would please a child of six. But I still remembered mainly my terror, which he never seemed to have noticed, except as it affected the schedule. From Father's diary of a weekend trip made May 20–21, 1949, to Washington, D.C.: "3:30 p.m.: Mt. Vernon. 4:45 p.m.: returned to Shoreham Hotel. Supper: Adam was sick, lost his supper. . . ."

With his two young grandsons, though, Father's ties were wholly different. It was really when David, the oldest, was born, that my own relationship with Father began to change. I no longer dreaded his visits. We seldom argued. He had eyes mainly for his grandchildren now, and I loved it. For the first time in my life, his attention was no longer on *me,* and on what he thought were the errors I was making in my life. As a result, my old, recurrent nausea completely disappeared, as mysteriously as it had arrived some twenty years before. It was as if I no longer needed that barrier between us. Perhaps the phobia had not been so irrational after all.

It was not only our children who eased his attitude toward me. There was something else, which he became aware of only gradually. Although I had not followed the life path he had fantasized for me, he began to notice that few of his friends' children or grandchildren had done so either. Many went through two or three marriages. Others, casualties of a new, competitive era in education, couldn't get into Yale or Princeton and went instead to colleges no one had ever heard of in West Virginia or Texas. Others became followers of various messiahs, Oriental and otherwise. So you say young Johnny's at . . . Cartwright College? And doing . . . Christian work? I welcomed all these departures from familiar paths. The more divorces, the more gurus, the better! It made my own life's course look quite reasonable by comparison, and some of Father's disapproval evaporated. At least I wasn't in an ashram.

Despite Father's initial certainty that both endeavors were big mistakes, my marriage turned out quite the contrary, and the magazine I co-founded, *Mother Jones,* became successful enough so that readers appeared even among the younger guests at Eagle Nest. One day he took Arlie aside and fumblingly acknowledged he had been wrong on the first count. On the second, he never said anything directly, but he started giving gift subscriptions to friends.

With less of Father's criticism to fend off, my life felt better to me, too. I enjoyed being an editor, and when I wrote, it seemed that it was in a voice that was my own. My life's course felt less a denial—I will *not* be the crown prince of Eagle Nest—and more an affirmation. Writing no longer seemed like acting a role, while I risked having my origins discovered at any moment. I grew more at ease with both parts of my identity. An old Eagle Nest paperweight of burnt-red African copper reappeared on my desk; by its side was another, given me by a typesetter friend, made of printer's lead.

Father visited us in California with clockwork regularity. About every six weeks he arrived on a Thursday evening on American Airlines flight 257, and left the following Monday night on TWA flight 44. Able to be a little more informal, he no longer wore a suit and tie while traveling. At the airport he was easy to recognize from far off: his short, broad-shouldered figure was a little stooped now; in all seasons he wore the same worn grayish-tan overcoat, his hands clasping the lapels in a gesture at once proprietary and anxious. He beamed and threw his arms wide as his two grandsons raced to meet him.

Only rarely did he show them that disapproving side. Once, coming home with him from the airport, David hit a toy against the car window, and Father told him a long, complicated story about a little boy who hit a window with a toy and broke the glass, and how this led to ambulances, policemen, hospitals, and so on. But the story just ran off David like rain off a leaf.

At times our children were uninterested in the toys that Father brought them. For them, his main gifts were those of self and time and attention. And these they had from him in abundance. When visiting us, he went to their schools and soccer games, read to them and told them stories by the hour.

He also went several times to the sociology courses Arlie taught at Berkeley. Highly popular, her lectures were often filled to capacity, and she had to turn students away.

"How'd you get into this class?" a student sitting next to Father asked. "I thought it was full."

"I've got influence with the management," Father replied.

At night he sang the children a German lullaby (*"Schlaf, Kindchen, schlaf"*) he remembered from his childhood, and lullabies in his other languages as well, sometimes singing himself to sleep before them. He did not analyze the details of their growth or new interests or skills, the things which would have fascinated my mother. It was enough that they cared for him, smiled at him, loved *him* with open arms and squeals of welcome. When he got these, he always shot a proud glance at me to be sure I had noticed.

He wrote for Gabriel, our younger child, a long, beautiful story about two horses who talked to each other about what they saw. He waded into a brook at Eagle Nest with David and helped him float a homemade boat downstream. And sometimes, riding in a car with both of them, he would burst spontaneously into song, "California, here I come . . . " None of these things, none at all, do I ever remember his doing with me. Was all this love there for me as a child and had I just not seen it? Was this—and not the other side—the real Father? Or perhaps the two of them were wound together, as intertwined as colored swirls in a candy cane.

It was only now, in his eighties, that Father put up in his study a picture of his own father, Berthold Hochschild, as if it had taken this long to come to terms with this formal, forbidding figure. Berthold had died long before I was born, but I started now to become curious about him. I sensed that in him I would have been able to see, in its purest form, everything about Father which had in the past made me stiff and uneasy. To know more about Berthold would be to follow a thread back to its point of origin.

Father and Gertrude had seldom talked about him when I was growing up, but now I urged Father to do so. I questioned other people who had known Berthold as well. I learned, for instance, that he had been perpetually constipated. He was also prone to terrible headaches, and when suffering from one he would have to lie down for several hours in a darkened room. People tiptoed about the house fearfully; Berthold would erupt in anger at any sound that disturbed him. He expected his children to live at home until they married, and was shocked and upset when Father, in his thirties, got an apartment of his own in New York. And he kept his small change neatly stacked in a bureau drawer. "The quarters in one pile, the dimes in another, the nickels in another. The heads all up, the tails down. And the faces on the coin heads all upright."

One day was still permanently branded on Father's memory seventy years later:

"Once when I was a teenager I took out an Eagle Nest motorboat without permission. On the other side of the lake the engine stalled and would not start again. My father let me drift all afternoon before he sent someone to tow me back. He barely spoke to me for the rest of the week."

Another occasion I heard about from both Father and another relative. Once a group of cousins from Germany were visiting New York. A party of a dozen or so young people, including Father and Gertrude, went out to an amusement park for the evening. Berthold told them to be back by ten. They had a marvelous time. Coming home on the subway, they realized they would be late. They worried more and more, spoke less and less. They hurried out of the subway stop and walked toward the house, terrified into complete silence. From two blocks away, they could see Berthold silhouetted in the front window, waiting, pocket watch in hand.

XXI

It is strange how, even when you feel you have understood something completely and have arranged your life accordingly, you continually see new layers, things that might seem obvious to an outsider but which you never noticed before. So it has been for me with Father and his world, the world of Eagle Nest.

Once, in California, I pick up my three-year-old son at the day-care home where he goes each day. It is a hot afternoon; he and the other children are still having their daily nap. And so I, too, lie on a couch in the baby-sitter's house, to doze until he awakens. Through the prism of that heightened awareness which sometimes comes as the child-self familiarity of sleep is juxtaposed with the adult-self strangeness of unfamiliar surroundings, I hear the noise of a lawn mower, which I have heard often enough over the years but not considered before. Floating in time, I now seem to hear all the dimensions of that sound for the first time. Here, someone on this street of sunbaked one-story stucco homes is mowing a lawn with a hand mower. There, at Eagle Nest, a much larger mower, one that pulled a driver on a wheeled seat behind it, cut the grass in the afternoon at nap time—each day all summer, it seemed, because there was so much grass to be mowed. And so I heard the mower as I napped or read through a thousand summer afternoons.

Now, this afternoon, near the shore of San Francisco Bay, it occurs to me that so many of the very sounds at Eagle Nest, sounds which can produce a burst of nostalgia in me still, were the sounds of other people laboring to make the place run for my benefit. Often, when the extra "help" hired for the summer did not work in the Club House itself, I did not even know their names. The sound, then, of the lawn mower. The sound of the whining chain saw in the woods, cutting up trees which had blown down and were blocking a riding trail. The sound of the larger circular saw in the work shed that cut that wood into fireplace lengths. The sound of the work-booted steps of whoever was this summer's handyman bringing the wood up the staircase from the cellar woodpile to the hearth.

Although it took a long time to sink in, growing up in such surroundings was the best political education I could have had. I did not need leftist theorists to convince me that class is the great secret everyone wants to deny: of course there was a ruling class; Father belonged. I did not need C. Wright Mills to point out the subtle links between business and government: I knew the man at The Company who had written a confidential report for President Kennedy on what his Africa policy should be; and John Foster Dulles at the State Department and his brother Allen at the CIA had come from The Company's law firm. I did not need Marx to show me that a person's very character is formed by, and cannot be separated from, class, power, possessions. I could not imagine Father without money, without The Company, without Eagle Nest. Could anyone?

As I grew older, I became more accustomed to this

way of looking at life. What I mean by that is an ever-clearer perception of how the joys, the power, and the riches of the world are divided so unfairly: between classes, between countries, between races, between men and women. When you feel the injustice of that division in one category—and for me it was the first—then your eyes begin to open to the others as well.

Looking back from that vantage point, I came to feel better about my painful shyness as a boy, about the uncomfortable nine- or ten-year-old who slouched down in the limousine's seat in order not to be seen by friends, or who was embarrassed by having half a dozen household servants when others had none. He was not just neurotically self-conscious, as his parents said. He had, instead, sensed some of the barriers that riches and poverty erected between himself and other human beings. He was on to something. He was right.

Even as I became more confident of where I stood, it was still difficult for me to know how to see Father in the light of what I now believed. He defied easy categorization.

On one side of the ledger, the more I learned about the whole system which underlay the abundance I had grown up with, the more I saw that wealth as plunder. The First World has been profiting from the Third for a long time, but mining raises this process to a new dimension, for it takes away from under the earth something which can never be replaced. And sometimes, particularly with strip-mining, it can destroy the land's surface as well. Often the land The Company mined was in distant countries, belonging to indigenous peoples ill-equipped to resist an onslaught of lawyers, engineers, drills, and bulldozers. Like all big mining corporations,

The Company profited particularly in Africa and Latin America because it could pay workers there only a small fraction of what they would earn in the United States.

At the time I was growing up, for example, black miners at The Company's vast Tsumeb mine in Namibia earned less than a dollar a day. The mine was worked by the infamous contract labor system, in which miners must leave their families behind for nearly a year at a time. Thousands of them finally went on strike in 1971–72; the police shot several dozen, and locked up hundreds of men and women in tightly packed steel cages and tortured them with electroshock.

To such facts Father and other Company officials always had ready responses: "Well, *that* particular mine is managed by another company in the joint venture, and we don't always see eye to eye with them." Or: "The Company has to operate under the laws of whatever country we're in, however much we may dislike them." Or: "But over in Zambia, of course, it's quite a different story, and we've been able to do some extremely progressive things." Or: "These mines are giving jobs to people who otherwise wouldn't have any." Every one of those statements was true. But still: how many black miners died to make life at Eagle Nest possible? In Namibia, The Company did not even pay compensation to miners who contracted silicosis—an incurable lung disease that can lead to early death.

Having seen this much of Father's world, I found it temptingly easy to say that my own course in life was simply a principled rebellion against it. For many years this was how I saw things. I had, I thought, changed sides. Wasn't he an executive in a rapacious industry? He was even The Company's chairman. And wasn't I the muckraking journalist, in solidarity with the oppressed everywhere? For here I was, marching in the antiwar demonstrations of the sixties, hearing the hollow crack of police billy clubs on human skulls, feeling in my nostrils the acrid bite of tear gas. And when I ringingly spoke to crowds at protest rallies, I took a secret pleasure in beginning with the words "Brothers and Sisters!"

But everything was not so simple. For, despite how The Company made its money, in his way of thinking Father was strikingly different from most businessmen. Unlike them, he had no hostility toward higher taxes, welfare, regulation, or labor unions. He never mouthed the common pieties about free enterprise. The corporate exposés I edited for *Mother Jones* didn't bother him, even when one mentioned a Company strip mine. He formed lasting friendships with black independence leaders in central Africa at a time when few other whites did so. And when the Vietnam War came along, the issue which most divided my generation from its parents, Father opposed the war from the start. In 1964, he wrote to *The New York Times* saying that the United States was suffering from "the delusion of omnipotence" in Vietnam, like Hitler in Europe, and that we should get out completely.

A few years later, a successor of his as chairman of The Company asked him to make a campaign contribution to a United States Senate candidate who had promised various favors to the mining industry. Father refused, because the man supported the Vietnam War. When Father began contributing money to various antiwar candidates, Lyndon Johnson, using his famous arm-twisting, invited him to dinner at the White House. Father went, but then supported peace candidates more generously than ever.

In the wake of Watergate, it was revealed that President Nixon had an "enemies list." Father was on it. He told a newspaper reporter he felt flattered.

What is one to make of such a man? Father never fully resolved the contradiction in himself, or even perceived it as such. He lived out both sides of it all his life: aristocrat, capitalist, important figure in the American empire; but at the same time a man with a distinct sense of social justice and a rare ability to see clearly. To that second side of him, I owe much—perhaps even the strength to rebel against the first.

Nowhere did Father's sense of justice show more clearly than in his feelings about China, where he had spent two years as The Company's representative in the 1920s. He always spoke so scornfully of the regime of Chiang Kai-shek that for a long time I wondered if someone in it had once slighted him personally. Had somebody not written him a thank-you letter? But nearly sixty years later, Arlie, who can get people to say things they never have said before, got Father to talk into a tape recorder about his life in China. A whole range of experience he had seldom mentioned came pouring out. He talked about his travels into the interior, by foot, sampan, and horse. He told of sleeping in farmers' huts, on the stone floors of Buddhist monasteries, and between opium-smoking boatmen on the open deck of a riverboat at night. He told of meeting a group of grieving peasants on a country road. A new warlord had sent his soldiers to collect taxes from them, five years in advance: "The peasants had nothing left to give, so the soldiers took their wives and daughters, whom these peasants expected never to see again."

For years after the Revolution of 1949, Father tried in vain to visit China again. When he was eighty, he succeeded, traveling there on one of the first delegations to visit the country as the thaw in U.S.-Chinese relations was beginning. In judging any social upheaval, most people generalize from the experience of their own class. But even though Father's old Chinese businessman friends and their families had lost everything, he came back from the trip still convinced that on the whole the Revolution had been a big step forward.

A few years later, some old letters turned up which Father had written home from China in the 1920s. Here is a passage from one:

> The glamour and romance that surround China, as depicted in American plays and books, vanish as soon as you . . . see the wretched poverty in which the bulk of the people live. . . . It would surprise you to see the absolute ignorance of the vast majority of Americans in particular, and of foreigners here in general, of all things Chinese. I've written you . . . already about the inane life that most of these people live, surrounded by such luxuries as the East affords. . . .
>
> One can discern beneath the maneuverings of the militarists and the bosses and the politicians and the reformers the faint stirrings of a consciousness on the part of the people that they have the power to throw out the predatory gang that are fighting among themselves for the control of the land. . . .

Was I the class rebel, or was he?

XXII

More than a decade out of college now, I perpetrate the great fraud that I am an adult. I have all the props to prove it: wife, children, house, career, the nursery school car pool to drive tomorrow morning. But by night I know differently. Though I am a continent's width away, in California, my dreams are usually of Eagle Nest. Even today I dream of Eagle Nest still, often on the first night after arriving in a foreign country.

In one dream I turn the place into a museum; there are charts and placards everywhere: they say how much everything costs and where the money comes from. In another, the highway on the other side of the lake, now well hidden behind a quarter-mile of forest, is rerouted along the shore, so people in their campers and vans can park and look out at us, across the water.

Then there are many dreams in which Eagle Nest is invaded—by foreign soldiers, by thousands of rats and mice. Or I dream that the superintendent comes to me, deeply distraught; there are hundreds of picnickers, campers, camera-bearing tourists all over the place, setting up their tents everywhere; he cannot keep them out.

In other dreams everything is rearranged. I find a whole new wing of rooms in the Club House which I had not known about before. Roads and riding trails are now in tunnels. New mountains rise up where there were none. The placid blue lake is transformed into a river, a torrent of white-green foam gouging out coves and lapping at the very porches of the houses. I dream that Berthold's fortune was founded on locks. I dream that I am part of a scientific experiment to find new uses for copper.

And then, finally, on a visit to Eagle Nest when I am well into my thirties, I sleep a sleep so dreamless and deep that when I wake I have forgotten where I am, and for an instant have even forgotten at what point I am in my life's arc. Above me I see the morning sun on the wooden ceiling of my old room. Now beside me is another's body, still asleep, warm, slender, soft, a swath of brown hair across a bare shoulder. I feel filled with love, desire, and, above all, wonder: I am in the same bed where slept the lonely little boy who heard voices on the lake late at night. Can I be the same person, inhabiting the same body, but no longer alone? Can I? Can I? It seems a miracle.

In Ingmar Bergman's great film *Wild Strawberries,* an old man near the end of his life revisits his childhood summer home. The house is deserted. He wanders through it. Then he falls asleep in a strawberry patch nearby and dreams of the old days. He dreams his way through the deep shade of a forest, through a tangle of thick underbrush, and at last reaches a lake shore. Frail and gray-haired, peering through the bushes, he sees his young parents fishing from a dock in the bright sunlight, wearing turn-of-the-century white summer clothes and straw hats, waving and smiling at him. Why does this moment of that film move me so deeply? It is as if the man can see his past clearly at last, but only after an en-

HALF THE WAY HOME

tire lifetime of trying. I am not yet old: can I see Father clearly? I am not sure. I did not feel I could even begin to do so until after he was dead. For the moment, then, I must jump ahead in time.

April 1982. On the drive north into the Adirondacks the opposite side of the highway is filled with trucks piled high with logs, coming down from the mountains. The highway climbs uphill; beside it appear the whitewater rapids that are the headwaters of the Hudson. Montreal draws closer; the rental car radio begins picking up rapid, static-laden French. The very distance I am going adds to the feeling of coming home. At last comes the glimmer of a frozen lake in the moonlight, and then the most welcome sound in the world, the slow crunch of gravel under the tires: the Eagle Nest driveway. For a moment it is as if the last twenty years have been erased: I am coming home from school or college for a winter weekend; my parents are waiting for me at the Cottage; ahead there are delicious long days of sleeping late, riding, reading by the fire, skiing in the woods.

When I was a boy I assumed, my parents assumed, everyone assumed, that Eagle Nest would go on forever the way it was. I would grow up, take Father's place, and someday become "Mr. Adam" to the servants. "I hope you marry a girl whose family goes to the mountains," my mother would say, a universe of assumptions in a single sentence. "Wouldn't it be dreadful if she liked the sea!"

But in his last years Father saw, reluctantly, that all this was not to be. Though he would have much preferred that we live on at Eagle Nest in his style, he provided in his will that the Club House become a writers' colony and conference center. In a few weeks from now it will open in its new incarnation as a public institution.

Father has been dead for some months. This will be my last visit to Eagle Nest for a long time, my last ever while the Club House is still a private home. It does not feel that way, however, for now each familiar tree, each bend in the road as I draw closer to the house, brings on the same feeling it always has. Eagle Nest will always be here; it will be at the end of every journey. Just as it appeared magically for Boris from the ashes of the Russian Revolution, and was here, unchanged, for Father when he returned from World War II, so, my feelings tell me against all reason, Eagle Nest will always be here for me, will survive even nuclear war itself.

Ostensibly I am coming here to finish the job of sorting and disposing of Father's possessions. But in fact it is to run my hands over the knotty-pine walls once more, to see the icy lacework of melted and refrozen snow on the tree branches, to hear the silence of the Eagle Nest winter.

It is dark, but I can still find the path and feel my way to my old room in the Cottage. Entering it, I feel ghostlike. On my other arrivals here over the years the house lights have been visible from far off; a fire has been burning; on my old desk has been a pile of clippings and letters and photos my mother has saved for me; my parents have been waiting. Now the only sound comes from outside, where under a half-moon the ice on the lake creaks and snaps and groans, preparing to break up and flow downstream in the spring days ahead.

I light the fire, then roam through the rooms. What moves me most are all the signs of my mother. One is an upstairs closet, smelling of leather and mothballs. Its walls are papered with funny pictures of furry animals, which she clipped from newspapers or *Life* magazine, with an eye to amusing a child: yawning seals, nuzzling hippos, elephants with trunks entwined, pigs wallowing in mud. Though my mother died seven years before him, Father never put away her bathing suit, a modestly old-fashioned one with a short flared skirt, which still hangs in its customary spot on the bathroom wall. In other rooms of the house are more photographs she taped up: pictures of Eagle Nest in winter, on days when the snow-drifts were higher than a person's head, days when the thickness of snow on the roofs emphasized the comfort of the house, the warmth of the fire inside. And finally the photos put up by Father after she died: pictures of my mother, young, smiling gently, on skis, rowing a boat, canoeing, climbing mountains in blue jeans with a pack on her back; a picture of her swimming in a lake at the foot of a volcano, on their honeymoon. This lithe, radiant woman, can she be the invalid I knew?

In Father's study, Berthold's mustachioed face gazes at me sternly from a small frame on the bureau. But I am unexpectedly touched at how many signs of me there are in this place. A lamp and drawings I made as a child. Books I recommended Father read, with the creased spines that show he really read them. A book I coauthored. Extra copies—to give away to people?—of a magazine article I wrote that won a prize. I remember the people who have written me in these last few months, in one of those stock phrases of condolence letters, "Your father was so proud of you." I mentally dismissed that each time: I knew the truth; they did not. Perhaps, I think now, they knew something I did not.

As I sit and wonder about this, I notice that I am in his pose: elbow on chair arm, first and second fingers bracketing my mouth, as if holding in my words before letting them out in a definitive judgment. In how many other ways as well am I now like him? Will my children feel toward me as I did toward Father, and he toward Berthold? Or have I broken that chain at last? I have my hopes, but cannot answer those questions yet. I hear their echo every time I become aware of one of those little ways in which I resemble Father. Each time someone points one out, it unnerves me: a few months ago an old friend of his wrote: "I was startled recently to hear Harold's voice on a radio program. But at the end of it, the announcer said I had been listening to you."

I go to bed beneath the thick, red Hudson's Bay Company blankets with their bold black stripes. The radiators make the same strange wheezing gurgle they have for forty years. The curtains hang on black iron rings, which, scraping along rods of the same metal as my mother pushed the curtains open, made the sound that heralded morning. The ceiling of my old room is stained from one cold winter night many years ago when the furnace failed, the pipes burst, and she went around lighting roaring fires in all the fireplaces.

All my adult life I have told myself, my parents, my friends, that it was wrong, outrageous, that one family should possess this whole property. And that was no pose; I felt it. I feel it now, more strongly than ever. As a reporter, I have been inside cinder-block migrant workers' barracks in South Africa, political prisoners' cells in El Salvador, the homes of black-lung miners in Appalachia. And I know now, as I did not when I was a child, just how the snow-covered balsam trees outside the window are rooted, in the end, beneath the scorched red earth of southern Africa. How, given all that, could I feel rightfully entitled to all that is here? I cannot. But can it be that in two more days I will leave, never to return to the Eagle Nest that once was? That seems impossible. I feel at home. From the air, where the smoke of his cremation has carried him, Father says: I told you so.

In the morning, I have much else I should do, but am drawn back to Father's study. Outside the window the bright sun reflects dazzlingly off the snow-covered ice on the lake. Across Father's desk, the chairs, all the surfaces of the room are spread rivers of paper from all parts of his life, flowing together here, to be sorted and then taken away for storage in a waiting pile of cardboard cartons. There are birth records in Hebrew and German from Berthold's native village, Eagle Nest account books that show oats and hay purchased for the stable, mining correspondence about drifts and shafts and stopes, a menu from The Company's fiftieth-anniversary dinner, printed on cardboard-thin sheaves of copper. And there are, among the copies of his own letters that he thought important enough to keep, a remarkable number scolding somebody for something: Boris for squandering Gertrude's money, a friend for not buckling down and working harder, a business partner for drinking too much, a young friend for having a too-stormy love affair. Often the letters end with that phrase I remember all too well: "I shall not speak of this again." So I was not the only target. I wish I had known that long ago.

I also reread some of the letters people wrote me after Father died. A surprising number of them show that thread of gifts and thanking that laced through his entire life. One letter is from the chairman of a department at Princeton, scarcely one of the country's needier universities. He tells how he had met Father socially soon after my parents had moved to Princeton; Father had taken him aside and asked him whether there was some way his department—not the university generally, but *his* department—could use some extra money? Now, many years later, this professor is sending me a handwritten, itemized accounting of how this puzzling and unexpected gift had been spent.

What lay behind that anxious compulsion of Father's to turn every relationship into one of donor and receiver? It seems almost as if he felt he had something to atone for—not a specific sin, but something deeper, some very state of being. I remember the way he was always so worried about inadvertently offending someone. There was a certain expression that rushed to his face at such moments: a guilty, abashed, shaken look as he said, "Oh I'm sorry, I'm so sorry." In a rare moment of confession, Father once told me that all his life he had had a recurring dream, of being trapped while climbing a cliff, unable to move up or down.

Among the papers on Father's desk is what may be a clue to the nature of that cliff he felt he was climbing. It is a memorandum typed on a dozen pages of now-brittle paper. I found it after Father died, at the back of a file cabinet in New York. I glanced through it quickly at the time, was puzzled, and made a mental note to look at it more closely. Now I do so. And, with mounting fascination, I begin to see how key a part of the puzzle it is. It is the missing piece.

The memo was written by Father in 1940, apparently just to share his thoughts with one or two friends. A short, noncommittal note from one, thanking him for "your interesting ideas on this subject" is the only other piece of paper in the same file. In the memo, Father asks whether the United States, like Germany, is heading for a great pogrom.

That was an important question to be asking in 1940. But a major, astounding point of Father's memo is that if a wave of anti-Semitism sweeps over the United States, it will be the "shortcomings" of the Jews themselves which are partly responsible. He talks about Jews who are too "loud," about low ethical standards in Jewish-dominated trades. He declares: "It is an unhappy fact, acknowledged by members of what may be termed the Jewish intelligentsia to each other but not to Gentiles, that a large proportion of the Jews in America are not properly educated to American business and social standards."

Above all, Father seems rattled by Jews who call attention to themselves: "Anyone who visits restaurants, theaters, or other places of entertainment in New York especially on Saturday or holiday nights, who has traveled on large pleasure-cruise ships, or who has seen certain types of Jewish summer hotels or camps near similar Gentile resorts must admit that differences in behavior play a part in anti-Semitism. . . . It may not be morally wrong for Jewish women to overdress and overload themselves with jewelry and makeup, but these habits are certainly repugnant to many Gentiles."

This reminds me of Father's constant disdain for people he called "flashy, Miami Beach types," and it suddenly occurs to me: Miami Beach is a *Jewish* resort.

What, Father asks in his memo, is to be done about all this? "Jews should lose no opportunity to convert the better-bred and better-educated Gentile minority to a friendlier attitude. . . . If Jews can win the respect or at least the tolerance of such Gentiles, the spread of active anti-Semitism will be impeded." At least the tolerance.

Perhaps this explains why Eagle Nest guest lists over the years were almost entirely WASP.

At last I feel I have come upon one key source of Father's sense of shame, awkwardness, vulnerability. For him being Jewish meant the constant risk of being mocked and condemned. And this was so even though neither he nor any of his immediate ancestors ever *were* persecuted. Yet the risk still remained there in his mind, a looming, crippling threat that could be unleashed at any time. Why, having encountered so little prejudice in his life, did he feel that threat so keenly? Of course one could argue that discrimination is subtle, and that history should teach any Jew to be wary, even a twentieth-century New Yorker. But Father's guilt-ridden anxiety went far beyond anything so rational. In it I see the scars left by his own father's outbursts of anger.

That letter from the Princeton professor, and lists of Father's other gifts, are still sitting on the desk before me. Suddenly everything fits into place. Father's defense against both real and imaginary anti-Semitism was to always be the donor. That was his urgent attempt to prove that he was not the hard-bargaining Jewish shopkeeper, not the verbally aggressive Jew of Yiddish humor, not the "loud" Jew he describes in his memo. His compulsive giving was a denial, a desperate plea: *I'm not one of them! No, no! Not at all! Accept me! Accept me! Look— here's a present for you!*

At the end of his memo, Father says: "Young Jews should be told frankly that certain Jewish tendencies are regarded by Gentiles as anti-social; they should be made to realize the advantages of unobtrusiveness." Unobtrusiveness. Young Jews. I was born two years after he wrote this. Today, as I reread the memo sitting in his Eagle Nest chair, those words are a beam of light from the past. Of all my childhood crimes in his eyes, the one most certain to draw a summons to this very desk for a reprimand was that of talking too much when there were guests present. Was I, in Father's eyes, acting too Jewish?

XXIII

After Father outlived his sparring partner at his New York club, he continued working out on a punching bag. In the daily diary he kept, he entered little symbols referring to what kind of exercise he had done each day—boxing, swimming, riding—and for how long. In his beloved Cottage at Eagle Nest, he moved about dressed in slippers or riding boots and his favorite ragged suede jacket. A few additional rooms and nooks added over the years gave the Cottage a comfortably ramshackle air, with the wood aged to different shades in different places. A disheveled clutter of books and magazines expanded over time to fill all available space. Father read, worked at his desk, and looked at the *Times* for much of each day—he always went through the paper once in the morning, and then again, more slowly, in the evening. He watched the TV news every night, but, never at ease with any piece of machinery, he took half a minute to turn the set off, pulling knobs that should be turned, turning buttons that should be pushed.

Just as our relationship had lacked a central dramatic scene of violent conflict, so, too, did it lack one of resolution. Neither of us said anything. There was no distinct turning point. Instead, I gradually became aware of an absence of tension, a certain ease in being with him. We developed running jokes to which we added a new layer of news and anecdote each time we met: about an eccentric relative, about words the children invented, about which of us had the greatest prowess with schedules and timetables.

Father's trips to California continued. When we lived in a small apartment in Berkeley, he stayed at a hotel when visiting us. When our second child was born, we moved to a house in San Francisco. Always uncomfortable at being someone else's guest, Father at first did not want to stay with us, even though it was a pleasant house with an extra bedroom. Reluctantly, he agreed to try. But after that first visit, he sent us a big box of particular kinds of towels, soap, and canned soup that he liked, as if symbolically to claim a part of our house as his own. From then on, he was happy there.

A few weeks before his eighty-eighth birthday, Father was out riding at Eagle Nest. His horse was frightened by an unfamiliar pile of newly cut brush at the roadside, and refused to walk past it. Instead of making a detour, Father, with his usual determination, forced the horse forward. It reared and he fell off: bruises, a concussion, several cracked bones. Somehow, using his great reserves of strength, he managed to fly to New York and walk into a hospital there. He jauntily wrote a friend: "The horse is in solitary confinement on bread and water for 30 days, but will be paroled when the cast is removed from my leg."

He hoped to be riding again soon. But this was not to be. Although we did not piece it all together until much later, the trauma of the fall accelerated a slow-growing lymph cancer he had apparently had for several years. He tried to carry on as usual, even taking half a dozen friends on a grand hotels tour of London, Paris, and Vienna. But he had to come back to New York early, in great pain.

There began some seven months of more pain, hospitals, doctors, physical therapy which didn't work, drugs of all kinds.

Surprisingly for such a robust man, Father had always taken many medicines. Not in a fearful, hypochondriacal way, but in an impatient way: if he had a cold or ailment of any kind, he wanted a pill that would cure it, without delay. He would order something hand-delivered from the New York pharmacy he had patronized for seventy years; if he was out of town, he would have them send it special delivery. Or he would dose himself from the vast array of drugs, including several antibiotics, which he kept on hand, choosing among pills as casually as one would choose something to eat from the icebox. Since he kept outliving his doctors, they didn't complain. Father often took double the prescribed dose of whatever the medicine was, on the theory that this would work better, just as you are apt to get better service next time if you give the headwaiter twice the usual tip.

As he grows weaker, I go back and forth to the East Coast. Once my arrival takes him by surprise as he sits trying to read, wrapped in a blanket, and he greets me with a joyful slip of the tongue, "Why, *Norman!*" But I feel moved and pleased, for this was the name of his oldest and best friend, his college roommate, dead now for thirty years.

Father's horizons have now shrunk to difficulties of stomach and sleep and bowel, the horizons of a child. And yet, when, just as if I were taking care of one of my children, I help him bathe or shower or dress, I am again childlike myself, awed by the strength of his body, even shrunken and weakened as it now is, when for the first time in my life I weigh more than he. His shoulders are still boxing-strong, ox-wide; his body tapers down in size from there.

I help him interview to find a practical nurse. Just like the miners who came in from the countryside to dig copper in Africa, all the candidates, coming to earn what they can in the big city, are from outlying colonial territories: Jamaica, Honduras, Puerto Rico, rural North Carolina. Against the woman we hire, against doctors and physical therapists and hospitals, Father fights a protracted campaign. His goal, which none of them wants to allow him, is to travel to Eagle Nest for Christmas and New Year's, to be the host for one last time.

In New York he moves with agonizing slowness between doctors' appointments. Once we go out to dinner at his favorite restaurant. I remember eating here years ago, suffering through one of those sudden bouts of nausea, while Father's other guests told him how marvelous the food was. The restaurant had been started by a Frenchman who was in the Army with Father; the waiters still call Father *monsieur le colonel*. They bring him the lobster and Puligny he always orders, but now it is he, not I, who is unable to eat.

Over the protests of all the doctors, we set off on the six-hour drive upstate. Limousines and fur lap robes seem almost a mockery of comfort now, of the illusion that money can prolong life. Father's mind goes back to German, the language he spoke with his own father. When I ask how he feels, he uses a German word which he says means "all played out." Strangely, though, I find myself denying what is obvious, talking about what we will do when he is better, about plans for the next summer.

Father had grown more gregarious as he got older; the painful shyness of his youth had left him, and he had come to enjoy being surrounded by people. In recent years the New Year's weekend has become the big social event of the year at Eagle Nest. Increasingly the guests Father has asked have been what he calls "young people"—anyone up to forty, often the children, and lately the grandchildren, of his old friends. Everything in his life was always planned several months in advance, and this weekend's group had been invited long before, when he still thought he would recover. I try to talk him out of staging the house party, but he is adamant.

For some reason there are more guests than ever. It feels strange to find almost all of them my age or younger: mostly up-and-coming executives, Wall Streeters or corporate lawyers, variants of what he wanted me to become. Almost the whole weekend, though, Father stays at the Cottage, trying to answer some of the letters piled on his desk, or sometimes sitting holding his four-year-old grandchild Gabriel in his lap silently for long periods of time. "Gabriel," he says once, cupping his grandson's entire face in his two hands, "make me happy."

Gusts of wind blow plumes of powdery snow from the Club House roof like curls of white smoke. Inside, we are twenty-seven at table, the most, I think, for a decade or two. Father is determined that his illness not dampen the festivities, and on New Year's Eve itself, he asks me to phone around and invite over many neighbors, as has always been his custom. There is no more *kazachok,* the ebullient Russian squat-kick dance, but, to more modern music, many of us dance until two or three in the morning, defying the presence of death.

Father feels so weak he only once manages to come

from the Cottage to join the guests at the Club House for dinner. Thus this whole weekend, for the first and last time in that house, I am the host. I sit at the head of the table, clink my knife on my glass for silence, find out how many people want to go riding or snowshoeing or cross-country skiing, make announcements of various activities like a cruise director. One last time, I Get The Beer.

XXIV

1939. War clouds over Europe. Molotov and Ribbentrop clink glasses to celebrate their pact. Germany prepares for the roundup of the Jews. From the American Dust Bowl, thousands of destitute farm families stream westward. On a New York terrace, there is a dinner dance one balmy summer evening. Among the guests, though they do not know each other yet, are two friends of the hosts. He is in his late forties; intelligent, people say, but stiff and restrained, an eternal bachelor. She has a warm, gentle beauty that catches the eye, but, like him, is clearly destined to remain single; all her friends have long since married.

They are introduced; they call each other "Mr." and "Miss"; they dance a sedate foxtrot. What goes through his mind as he makes small talk with her? That she was impeccably Anglo, for sure; that she would be his final certificate of entry into that world (as, indeed, he was to make it into the *Social Register* a year after they married). And yet . . . there was much more, too. Some deep kindness in her face says: with me it is safe; with me you can take that step out of yourself you have not taken for nearly fifty years. After the party, he says something to the host, asking to be invited to dinner with her again: he was too shy to call her directly. Waiting for others to arrange their next meeting meant a months-long delay.

How impossibly hard it must have seemed to him to make that first call to her.

What were the mysteries that lay ahead of them in bed? For her, almost certainly they were mysteries; maybe they were for him, too; I still do not know. Whatever was to happen there, there are clues that it was good: a few shy, tender references in letters I was to find after they both were dead, even in letters written long after they had been married. Ahead of them lay all the proper forms of things: I was also to find, filled in neatly in her handwriting, a leather book, embossed in gold: "Wedding Presents," with ruled columns: "Gift," "From Whom," "Where Purchased," "Acknowledged," "Remarks"; it was mostly silver from Tiffany's and one or two other stores. And yet, if there were two people of their generation who better rescued each other from otherwise lonely lives, I never met them. Could any child ask for a greater gift?

1981. Three weeks after that final New Year's weekend at Eagle Nest. Once again, a hospital in New York. Father, my father, is here, and the doctors say he has little time left. As my mother, my protector, stayed with me for my ear operation when I was five, now I stay with Father. I feel as if it is *her* caring, her compassion, her love I am expressing toward him, for I feel in myself something less, or perhaps more complicated, than love. When I ask if he wants me to move into the hospital room with him, to my surprise—and to a flooding feeling almost of exhilaration: his need for me is greater than my fear of him—he says yes. And so I move in, sleeping on a cot, for the duration.

Just as I knew one of them would die abroad, so I knew

one would die here. Gertrude died in this hospital; a director of The Company is now dying across the hall. Just as there is Mother Teresa's famous Dying Home for the poor in Calcutta, so this hospital, with its windows looking out across the Hudson, is a Dying Home for the rich. On maps of Manhattan it appears as one giant hospital, but it is in fact two. Late at night when the wood-paneled entrance to the private pavilion is closed, you have to walk through the hospital for the poor to get to the hospital for the rich. Patients in the former are nearly all black or Hispanic; some fifty or sixty of them wait on folding metal chairs. Security guards stand about, bristling with straps and guns and billy clubs. There are curtained cubicles for seeing the doctor, dimly lit halls, a smell of stopped-up toilets. Painted arrows on the linoleum floor direct you where to stand in line. When he first came here some months ago after falling off the horse, Father had to wait five hours in this emergency room. His doctor found out about it the next day and raised hell: what had happened, of course, was that Father, being injured (only the poor get injured; the rich get ill), had been put in the hospital for the poor by mistake.

When you pass through a set of glass doors, you cross the frontier between the two hospitals. This floor, where Father is, is the most exclusive of all, with handsome wooden doors on the rooms, and a kitchen which prepares things like lobster tail and rack of lamb. Doctors come by frequently; the nurses—everyone has a private nurse—are not black, as they seem to be in the hospital for the poor, but Irish, with soft brogues. Above all, the rich have purchased the solicitousness of doctors, of nurses, even of hospital officials, one of whom, wearing a business suit, comes by like a restaurant owner, "just to make sure everything is all right."

We talk very little. Father has energy to do so only for a few minutes at a time. But his mind is totally clear. We reminisce about a few of those trips together when I was small. I read him an article I've just published; he says he likes it. And he tells me, for the first time, about something he did as a ten-year-old boy visiting Germany with his parents before World War I:

"I used to sneak off on Sunday afternoons to watch a cavalry band on parade. There was one part of Frankfurt where they did that. With the big kettledrums on either side of the saddle, and all that. My father didn't know. He wouldn't have approved. Jews were not allowed to become cavalry officers, you see."

I wonder: Is this where Father's lifetime passion for riding came from?

There is a smell of death about him now; no hospital deodorants or rubber gloves or absorbent pads can take it away. When he talks to me: "Adam, can you mop my forehead?" "Adam, can you get me my slippers?" I have a strange feeling that it is not *me,* now, he is talking to, but rather an imagined, childhood Adam, an Adam with all the emotions a son is supposed to have, not me as I am now. Then that feeling ebbs away; the two Adams collapse into one, as he says, "Adam, come sit by me for a while," the only time in his life he has made such a request.

He wakes and sleeps at intervals that have become disconnected from the flow of night and day. One night he wakes and says, "I'd like some vodka." There is none in the hospital. So I walk out, through the hospital for the poor, past the waiting room full of policemen and junkies and street-fight victims, to a liquor store. A continuous sheet of bulletproof plastic goes all the way to the ceiling;

you slide in your money and receive your pocket-flask bottle in a tray recessed in the counter.

Another time he wakes in the middle of the night and, conscientious to the end, dictates to me a letter answering a request for news from his college class secretary: ". . . I traveled to Europe in June. I continue in my interest in Adirondack history. . . . " Groans sometimes escape him, but when you look to inquire or comfort, he says, "Excuse me," as if he had involuntarily spoken out of turn.

He focuses on his movements from bed to chair and chair to bed: a huge effort each time, planned and coordinated between him and me and the nurse. At night, restless, he moves back and forth between the two more often. We succeed in getting him into bed; in a few minutes he wants us to lower its side railing so he can get out again, into the chair. That old, intimidating obstinacy flashes out:

"Take down the railing, please."

"Aw, but darlin', ye were just awp," the Irish nurse says. "Try t' sleep now."

"Take down the railing, please."

"Try t' sleep."

"Take down the railing."

We do.

Later, it is an effort for him even to move from one side to the other in bed. There are more groans, but he cannot name where it hurts. Tears collect in his eyes; he cannot move his head to let them drain; I wipe them away. What is the pain he is feeling? Is it exhaustion, something intensely painful in itself to someone who always felt boundless energy? Or is dying itself a hurt, a wound, not located in any part of the body, but pain of a sort different from anything the rest of us can imagine? I feel a rush of vertigo, an unexpected fear that this is not death as it is in novels and movies, not death in which one looks back on life and sees all things truthfully at last, not death as I've imagined my own death will be, no, no, not at all.

He begins to bleed internally; he vomits blood; there is blood everywhere. The nurses and I clean up; the doctor comes and gives pills, for God's sake. Father's eyes look like those of a wounded, cornered animal.

He sleeps. I eat a little dinner. There is a lull, a peacefulness. It seems as if the end will surely not come for at least a day or two. We will have time to talk more, maybe even to have, in abbreviated form, that conversation we have never had, about him and me. I sit beside him and hold his hand.

Suddenly the nurse hears some subtle change in breathing, something I can't hear, and quickly comes over with a stethoscope. His eyes fly open wide, staring up, not at me but through me. I have not cried since I was a teenager, but now a sob comes tearing up from an unknown territory inside me. My lips form around the essential, difficult "I love you." I think it is true. I think he can hear.

His breath comes in deep gasps, then subsides. I press my ear to his chest. Something; yes, definitely some sound still there. But the nurse tells me the heartbeat I'm hearing is my own.

ADAM HOCHSCHILD was born in New York in 1942. He first worked as a newspaper reporter for the *San Francisco Chronicle* and as an editor and writer for *Ramparts* magazine. Later he was one of the co-founders of *Mother Jones* magazine and was its first managing editor. His articles and reviews have also appeared in *Harper's, The New York Times, The Village Voice, The New Republic, The Nation,* and elsewhere. He has been a commentator on the National Public Radio program "All Things Considered." His work has won prizes from the Eugene V. Debs Foundation and the Overseas Press Club of America.